a year of GIFTS of good taste

*W*hy wait for a holiday to share a gift from your heart? Jam-packed with creative foods and crafty presentations, A Year of Gifts of Good Taste *features fun surprises for making any day special — and making special days extraordinary! For example, you can share the bounty of a summer garden with Tomato-Basil Jam delivered in a clever twig basket, celebrate Great American Pie Month with a creamy, dreamy treat, or send merry Christmas greetings with a decorated canvas stocking packed with Black Walnut Brittle. As you browse through the pages of this imaginative guide, you'll quickly discover that there are as many reasons to celebrate as there are days in the year!*

Anne Childs

LEISURE ARTS, INC.
Little Rock, Arkansas

a year of GIFTS of good taste

EDITORIAL STAFF

Vice President and Editor-in-Chief: Anne Van Wagner Childs
Executive Director: Sandra Graham Case
Design Director: Patricia Wallenfang Sowers
Foods Editor: Celia Fahr Harkey, R.D.
Editorial Director: Susan Frantz Wiles
Publications Director: Kristine Anderson Mertes
Creative Art Director: Gloria Bearden
Senior Graphics Art Director: Melinda Stout

DESIGN

Designers: Katherine Prince Horton, Sandra Spotts Ritchie, Linda Diehl Tiano, Rebecca Sunwall Werle, and Anne Pulliam Stocks
Executive Assistants: Billie Steward and Debra Smith

FOODS

Assistant Foods Editor: Jane Kenner Prather
Test Kitchen Home Economist: Rose Glass Klein
Test Kitchen Coordinator: Nora Faye Taylor
Test Kitchen Assistant: Tanya Harris

TECHNICAL

Managing Editors: Barbara McClintock Vechik and Kathy Rose Bradley
Technical Writers: Briget Julia Laskowski and Carol V. Rye
Technical Associate: Laura Lee Powell

EDITORIAL

Managing Editor: Linda L. Trimble
Associate Editor: Tammi Williamson Bradley
Assistant Editors: Stacey Robertson Marshall, Terri Leming Davidson, and Janice Teipen Wojcik

ART

Book/Magazine Graphics Art Director: Diane M. Hugo
Senior Production Graphics Artist: Michael A. Spigner
Photography Stylist: Karen Smart Hall

PROMOTIONS

Managing Editors: Alan Caudle and Marjorie Ann Lacy
Associate Editors: Steven M. Cooper, Dixie L. Morris, Jennifer Ertl Wobser, and Marie Trotter
Designer: Dale Rowett
Art Director: Linda Lovette Smart
Production Artist: Leslie Loring Krebs
Publishing Systems Administrator: Cindy Lumpkin
Publishing Systems Assistant: Susan Mary Gray

BUSINESS STAFF

Publisher: Bruce Akin
Vice President, Marketing: Guy A. Crossley
Vice President and General Manager: Thomas L. Carlisle
Retail Sales Director: Richard Tignor
Vice President, Retail Marketing: Pam Stebbins

Retail Marketing Director: Margaret Sweetin
Retail Customer Service Manager: Carolyn Pruss
General Merchandise Manager: Russ Barnett
Vice President, Finance: Tom Siebenmorgen
Distribution Director: Rob Thieme

Library of Congress Catalog Number 97-75960
International Standard Book Number 1-57486-105-0

Table of Contents

April Fools

The start of a new year is the ideal time to resolve to eat more soup! One of the world's most popular and versatile dishes, soup can be rich and creamy or thick and hearty like our Cheesy Potato-Sausage Soup. This savory mixture stirs sharp Cheddar cheese into a pot of seasoned veggies and Italian sausage. To fortify a friend after a day in the chilly outdoors, deliver a jar of soup topped with a simple felt cover. The matching snowflake place mats feature fused-on snowflakes and running stitch borders.

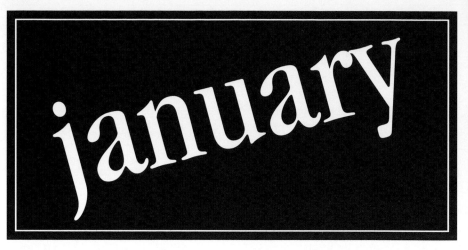

CHEESY POTATO-SAUSAGE SOUP

- 2 pounds potatoes, peeled and cut into 1-inch cubes (about 4¹/₂ cups)
- 3 cans (14¹/₂ ounces each) low-sodium chicken broth
- 1 pound Italian sausage
- 1 cup chopped celery
- 1 green pepper, coarsely chopped
- 1 sweet red pepper, coarsely chopped
- ¹/₂ cup chopped green onions
- 1 clove garlic, minced
- 2 tablespoons cornstarch
- ¹/₂ cup dry white wine
- 3 tablespoons chopped fresh parsley
- 2 teaspoons dry mustard
- 4 cups (16 ounces) shredded sharp Cheddar cheese

In a large Dutch oven, combine potatoes and chicken broth. Cover and cook over medium-high heat about 25 minutes or until potatoes are tender.

While potatoes are cooking, brown and crumble sausage in a heavy large skillet over medium heat. Add celery, peppers, green onions, and garlic; sauté about 15 minutes or until vegetables are tender. Drain sausage mixture.

In a small bowl, dissolve cornstarch in wine. Bring potato mixture to a boil. Add cornstarch mixture; stir until thickened. Stir sausage mixture, parsley, and dry mustard into potato mixture. Remove soup from heat. Add cheese; stir until melted. Serve hot. Store in an airtight container in refrigerator.

Yield: about 12 cups soup

SNOWFLAKE PLACE MATS AND JAR LID COVER

For each place mat, you will need a 13¹/₄" x 18" piece of red fleece, white felt, paper-backed fusible web, and white embroidery floss.
For jar lid cover, you will *also* need a 10" square of red fleece, and ⁵/₈ yd of 1³/₈"w ribbon.

1. For *each* place mat, use patterns, page 108, and follow *Making Appliqués,* page 123, to make one *each* of snowflake A and snowflake B appliqués, and two *each* of snowflake C appliqués from felt.
2. Arrange snowflakes on fleece piece; fuse in place.
3. Use floss to work *Running Stitch,* page 124, along edges of fleece to complete place mat.
4. For jar lid cover, refer to Step 1 to make desired snowflake appliqué. Center and fuse snowflake to fleece square. Center snowflake on top of lid. Knot ribbon length around lid.

NEW YEAR'S TOAST

*W*elcome the new year
*in festive style with sparkling
Raspberry Champagne Cocktails.
To create a ready-made party for
two, weave colorful ribbon
through a simple wooden crate,
then pack it with a bottle of
homemade raspberry syrup,
a bottle of bubbly, and a pair
of champagne glasses. Add a
fun gift tag to announce your
wishes for a "Happy New Year!"*

RASPBERRY CHAMPAGNE COCKTAILS

    2   cups frozen whole red raspberries
  $1/2$ cup sugar
  $1/2$ cup Chambord or other raspberry
         liqueur
  $1/3$ cup cognac
  $1/2$ teaspoon grated lemon zest
    1   bottle (750 ml) champagne

In a medium bowl, combine
raspberries and sugar. Cover and let stand
at room temperature 45 minutes, stirring
and mashing mixture occasionally.

In a 1-quart glass container, combine
raspberry mixture, liqueur, cognac, and
lemon zest; cover and let stand at room
temperature 3 days.

Strain mixture; discard seeds and
zest. Store raspberry syrup in an airtight
container in refrigerator. Give with serving
instructions.

Yield: about $1^1/2$ cups syrup

To serve: Place $2^1/2$ tablespoons raspberry
syrup in a 6-ounce champagne glass; fill
with chilled champagne. Serve
immediately.

"HAPPY NEW YEAR!" GIFT TAG

You will need a photocopy of tag design
(page 119); lavender paper; pink, green,
yellow, and lavender markers; lavender
permanent felt-tip pen; decorative-edge
craft scissors; and glue.

1. Use markers to color tag design. Use
pen to write message on tag. Cut out tag.
2. Glue tag to lavender paper. Leaving a
$1/4$" lavender border, use craft scissors to
cut out gift tag.

HOT TEA DAYS

*T*he chilly days of
January usher in 31 reasons
to enjoy our aromatic Herb
Tea Blend, a soothing and
relaxing beverage. A friend
who appreciates the simple
pleasure of sipping tea will
cherish a basket filled with
the tea and a pretty cup and
saucer. We trimmed our basket
with lovely plaid ribbon and
a spray of colorful posies.

HERB TEA BLEND

  3/4 cup loose tea leaves
  1/4 cup dried sage leaves
    3 tablespoons dried thyme leaves
    1 tablespoon dried lemon peel

Combine tea, sage, thyme, and lemon
peel in a resealable plastic bag. Give with
serving instructions.

Yield: about 1 1/4 cups tea blend

To serve: Place 2 teaspoons tea blend in a
teapot for every 8 ounces hot water used.
Pour boiling water over tea. Cover and
steep 3 to 5 minutes. Strain into tea cups;
serve with lemon slices and honey.

For folks who enjoy foods with a fiery nature, our Jalapeño-Black Bean Chili is a four-alarm culinary creation! The "More water, please!" dish — loaded with peppers, pork, vegetables, and herbs — makes a savory winter warmer. For a red-hot delivery, present a jar of chili tucked in a spatter-painted "recycled" can with sponged-on pepper motifs. Natural raffia, artificial peppers, and a fabric-covered gift tag wrap up your surprise.

JALAPEÑO-BLACK BEAN CHILI

Use mild jalapeño peppers unless you enjoy a very spicy chili. This recipe is also delicious made with chicken.

- 4 cloves garlic, minced
- 4 pound boneless pork loin roast
- 1 tablespoon all-purpose flour
- 1 jar (12 ounces) pickled jalapeño pepper slices
- 3 cups chopped onions
- 2 tablespoons vegetable oil
- 3 cans (15 ounces each) black beans
- 2 cans (15$\frac{1}{4}$ ounces each) whole kernel yellow corn, drained
- 2 cans (14$\frac{1}{2}$ ounces each) diced tomatoes
- 2 teaspoons ground cumin
- 1$\frac{1}{2}$ teaspoons salt
- $\frac{1}{4}$ cup chopped fresh cilantro

Preheat oven to 350 degrees. Rub garlic over roast. Sprinkle flour into a large oven baking bag. Place roast in bag. Pour undrained jalapeño peppers over roast. Close and pierce bag according to manufacturer's instructions. Insert meat thermometer, through bag, into thickest portion of roast. Bake 1 hour or until thermometer registers 160 degrees. Cool roast in bag about 45 minutes or until cool enough to handle. Reserving meat drippings and cooked peppers, transfer roast to a cutting board. Cut meat into small pieces. Skim fat from meat drippings.

In a large Dutch oven, cook onions in oil over medium-high heat about 10 minutes or until onions are tender and begin to brown. Reduce heat to medium. Stir in pork, reserved meat drippings and peppers, undrained beans, corn, undrained tomatoes, cumin, and salt.

Stirring occasionally, cover and simmer about 45 minutes. Stir in cilantro and cook 15 minutes longer. Serve warm. Store in an airtight container in refrigerator.

Yield: about 17 cups chili

PAINTED PEPPERS CONTAINER

You will need a 3-lb coffee can; white spray paint; yellow, red, green, and black acrylic paint; compressed craft sponge; small household paintbrush; tracing paper; natural raffia; and artificial peppers floral pick.

For gift tag, you will *also* need a 1$\frac{3}{4}$" x 3$\frac{1}{4}$" white paper piece; 2$\frac{3}{4}$" x 4$\frac{1}{4}$" piece *each* of fabric, paper-backed fusible web, and poster board; and a brown calligraphy pen.

Refer to Painting Techniques, page 123, for painting tips.

1. Spray paint can white.
2. To spatter-paint can, dip paintbrush into diluted yellow paint. Tap handle once to remove excess paint. Tap paintbrush over can as desired. Repeat using remaining colors of paint.
3. To sponge-paint can, trace patterns, page 108, on tracing paper; cut out. Trace around patterns on sponge; cut out shapes. Use shapes and follow *Sponge Painting*, page 123, to paint peppers on can.
4. Cut several lengths of raffia. Knot raffia around can. Insert peppers into knot.
5. For gift tag, use brown pen to write message on white paper piece. Fuse web to wrong side of fabric. Fuse fabric to poster board. Center and glue tag to fabric-covered poster board.

CHARMING CHEESE CRATE

After the harried holiday season, encourage an overworked "holiday-holic" to sit down and relax with a gift of creamy Honey-Mustard Cheese Spread. The slightly sweet appetizer blends three cheeses with a touch of honey. Decorated with stenciled motifs, a plain wooden crate makes a clever carrier for the cheese and crackers.

HONEY-MUSTARD CHEESE SPREAD

- 2 cups (8 ounces) shredded mild Cheddar cheese
- 1 cup (4 ounces) shredded sharp Cheddar cheese
- 2 packages (3 ounces each) cream cheese, softened
- 2 tablespoons honey
- 2 tablespoons chopped fresh dill weed
- 1 tablespoon finely chopped onion
- 1 tablespoon dry mustard
  Crackers to serve

Process cheeses, honey, dill weed, onion, and dry mustard in a food processor until well blended. Chill cheese spread in an airtight container overnight to let flavors blend. Serve at room temperature with crackers.

Yield: about 2¹/₃ cups cheese spread

STENCILED WOODEN CRATE

You will need an 8" x 14" wooden crate with handle, fabric piece to line crate, stencil plastic, craft knife and cutting mat, green and blue-green acrylic paint, stencil brushes, small paintbrush, natural raffia, brown permanent felt-tip pen, two small pinecones, and glue.

1. Use pattern, page 109, and follow *Stenciling,* page 123, to stencil green and blue-green trees on crate as desired.
2. Use pen to draw snowflakes on crate and to outline and draw detail lines on trees.

3. Use pen to draw triangles along side of handle. Paint top of handle and triangles green. Use pen to draw a grid pattern between triangles.
4. Tie several lengths of raffia into a bow around handle. Glue pinecones to bow.
5. Follow *Making a Basket Liner,* page 124, to make liner with an unfinished edge.

RELAXING COCOA MIX

A lighthearted occasion, National Nothing Day (January 16) was created "to provide Americans with one national day when they can just sit without celebrating, observing, or honoring anything." To encourage a friend's non-celebration of this novel event, share a gift of Spicy Cocoa Mix. The aromatic blend makes a delicious beverage to sip while relaxing and doing nothing — on any day! For a heartwarming finish, include a set of handy mitten coasters and a felt gift tag.

SPICY COCOA MIX

3¹/₂ cups firmly packed brown sugar
2 cups cocoa
2 teaspoons ground cinnamon
¹/₂ teaspoon ground nutmeg
¹/₂ teaspoon ground cloves
¹/₄ teaspoon salt

Process brown sugar, cocoa, cinnamon, nutmeg, cloves, and salt in a food processor until well blended. Store in an airtight container. Give with serving instructions.

Yield: about 5 cups cocoa mix

To serve: Pour 6 ounces hot milk over 1¹/₂ tablespoons cocoa mix; stir until well blended. Serve warm.

MITTEN COASTERS AND GIFT TAG

For each coaster, you will need three colors of felt (we used yellow, red, and blue), assorted buttons, tracing paper, pinking shears, and glue.
For gift tag, you will *also* need cream colored paper, black permanent felt-tip pen, hole punch, and a 12" length of jute twine.

1. Trace patterns, page 109, on tracing paper; cut out. Use patterns and felt to cut mitten front, mitten back, and heart; use pinking shears to cut cuff.
2. Glue mitten front, heart, and cuff to mitten back. Glue three buttons along cuff.

3. For gift tag, cut a 2" x 2¹/₂" piece from red felt. Cut a piece from cream paper slightly smaller than red felt piece. Use pen to write message on paper piece. Use pinking shears to trim short edges of paper piece. Center and glue paper piece to red felt. Glue red felt to yellow felt. Leaving a ¹/₄" yellow border, use pinking shears to cut out gift tag.
4. Punch hole in tag. Thread twine through hole and tie tag to gift.

13

ALL-STAR CHILI TOPPINGS

*D*raft our all-star lineup of chili toppings to score taste touchdowns at your game-watching party! The flavorful front line features Cheese Blend, Onion Relish, Mustard Relish, and Creamy Fresh Salsa. Team them up with your favorite chili to tackle even the heartiest of appetites. Jars of the condiments are huddled in a turf-lined basket that's decorated with pictures of the group's favorite team. Matching jar lids, a miniature pennant, and streamers in team colors lend spirit to this "fan-tastic" surprise!

GAME DAY CONDIMENTS

CHEESE BLEND

  1 cup (4 ounces) shredded sharp
      Cheddar cheese
  1 cup (4 ounces) shredded mild
      Cheddar cheese
  1 cup (4 ounces) shredded
      Monterey Jack cheese

Combine cheeses in an airtight container. Store in refrigerator.

Yield: about 3 cups cheese

ONION RELISH

  2 cups chopped onions
  1/2 cup apple cider vinegar
  1/2 cup sugar
  1/2 teaspoon salt
  1/4 teaspoon ground black pepper
  1/2 teaspoon celery seed
  1/2 teaspoon mustard seed
  1/4 teaspoon ground turmeric

In a medium bowl, combine onions, vinegar, sugar, salt, pepper, celery seed, mustard seed, and turmeric. Cover and store in refrigerator.

Yield: about 2 cups onion relish

MUSTARD RELISH

  1 1/2 cups prepared mustard
  1/2 cup drained hamburger dill pickle
      slices
  1/2 cup chopped sweet pickles
  1/4 cup drained pickled jalapeño
      pepper slices

Process mustard, pickles, and peppers in a food processor until mixture is coarsely chopped. Store in an airtight container in refrigerator.

Yield: about 2 cups mustard relish

CREAMY FRESH SALSA

  1 1/2 cups coarsely chopped and drained
      plum tomatoes (about 3 tomatoes)
  3 tablespoons chopped green onions
  3 tablespoons chopped green pepper
  3 tablespoons chopped fresh cilantro
  1 1/2 tablespoons finely chopped celery
  1 clove garlic, minced
  1/4 teaspoon salt
  1/8 teaspoon ground black pepper
  1/3 cup sour cream

In a medium bowl, combine tomatoes, green onions, green pepper, cilantro, celery, garlic, salt, and black pepper. Fold in sour cream. Cover and store in refrigerator.

Yield: about 2 cups salsa

TOUCHDOWN BASKET

You will need a cardboard box (we used a 6" x 13" box), football magazines, corded piping, green artificial turf, yellow and green curling ribbon, decoupage glue, foam brush, and glue.
For jar lid and flag, you will *also* need tracing paper, yellow and green paper, black permanent felt-tip pen, 10"l bamboo skewer, decorative-edge craft scissors, and glue.

1. Cut motifs from magazines. Use foam brush to apply decoupage glue to wrong side of each motif. Glue motifs around outside of box, overlapping motifs as desired; allow to dry.
2. Measure around top edge of box; add 1". Cut a piece of piping the determined measurement. Gluing raw edge to inside of box and overlapping ends, glue piping around top of box.
3. Refer to Fig. 1 and measure length of inside of box from rim to rim (shown in red); measure width of box (shown in blue). Cut one piece of turf the determined measurements. Glue to inside of box. Measure length and height of one long side of box. Cut two pieces of turf the determined measurements. Glue each piece to inside of box.

Fig. 1

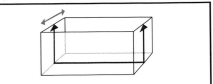

4. Cut several lengths of curling ribbon. Glue centers of ribbon lengths to top corners of box; curl ends.
5. For *each* jar lid, remove band from jar. Trace around inside opening of band on tracing paper; cut out. Use pattern to cut circle from turf. Glue circle to top of jar lid. Draw around tracing paper circle on yellow paper. Use craft scissors to cut out label 1/4" inside drawn line. Use pen to write recipe name on label. Glue label to turf circle.
6. For flag, trace pattern, page 110, on tracing paper; cut out. Draw around pattern on green paper. Use craft scissors to cut out flag. Refer to grey line on pattern to fold tab to back of flag. Glue one end of skewer into fold. Use pen to write message on flag. Cut several lengths of curling ribbon. Tie ribbons into a bow and glue bow to top of flag; curl ends.

We would not tell a lie — these Chocolate Cherry-Almond Creams are melt-in-your-mouth wonderful! And what better time to enjoy them than during the month of George Washington's birthday! Whimsical tins, accented with painted cherry motifs, silk leaves, and eye-catching ribbons, add flair to a gift of these yummy bites.

february

CHOCOLATE CHERRY-ALMOND CREAMS

1/2 cup butter or margarine, softened
1 can (14 ounces) sweetened condensed milk
1 teaspoon vanilla extract
1/2 teaspoon almond extract
11 cups sifted confectioners sugar
2 cups slivered almonds, toasted and finely chopped
1 jar (10 ounces) maraschino cherries, drained, chopped, and patted dry
24 ounces chocolate candy coating, chopped
1 package (12 ounces) semisweet chocolate chips

In a large bowl, beat butter until fluffy. Add sweetened condensed milk and extracts; beat until well blended. Gradually stir in confectioners sugar, kneading in last 4 cups. Knead in almonds and cherries. Shape mixture into 1-inch balls. Place on a baking sheet lined with waxed paper. Chill 2 hours or until firm.

In top of a double boiler, melt candy coating and chocolate chips over hot, not simmering, water. Placing each ball on a fork and holding over saucepan, spoon chocolate over balls. Place balls on baking sheet lined with waxed paper. Drizzle remaining chocolate over each candy to decorate. Chill candies about 10 minutes or until chocolate hardens. Store in an airtight container in refrigerator.

Yield: about 9 dozen candies

PAINTED CHERRY TINS

For each container, you will need desired size tin; assorted white and black ribbons; yellow spray paint; yellow, red, and black acrylic paint; paintbrushes; small silk leaves; tracing paper; transfer paper; and glue.

Refer to Painting Techniques, page 123, for painting tips.

1. Spray paint tin yellow; allow to dry.
2. Trace cherry pattern, page 110, on tracing paper. Use transfer paper to transfer design to top and sides of tin as desired.
3. Paint cherries red and highlights yellow. Use black paint to add stems.
4. Glue leaves close to cherries.
5. Glue or tie ribbon around tin or lid as desired.

MY FUDGY VALENTINE

*O*n Valentine's Day, sharing sweet wishes is easy when you offer our rich Valentine Cherry Fudge. Each bite of the creamy chocolate confection yields bits of yummy candied cherries. For a charming delivery, the fudge is placed on an easy-to-make decoupaged plate and then topped with a paper doily and a spray of ribbon-tied posies.

VALENTINE CHERRY FUDGE

- 1/2 cup butter or margarine
- 2 cups sugar
- 1 can (5 ounces) evaporated milk
- 1 package (12 ounces) semisweet chocolate chips
- 1 jar (7 ounces) marshmallow creme
- 2 packages (4 ounces each) candied red cherries, chopped
- 1 teaspoon vanilla extract

Grease a 9-inch-wide by 2-inch-deep heart-shaped pan. Line pan with aluminum foil, extending foil over sides of pan and keeping foil as smooth as possible; grease foil. In a heavy medium saucepan, combine butter, sugar, and evaporated milk. Whisking constantly, bring mixture to a full rolling boil over medium heat. Continuing to whisk constantly, boil 5 minutes; remove from heat. Stir in chocolate chips, marshmallow creme, cherries, and vanilla. Pour mixture into prepared pan; allow to cool 1 hour at room temperature. Chill 2 hours or until firm.

Use edges of foil to lift fudge from pan. Store in an airtight container in refrigerator.

Yield: about 3 pounds fudge

DECOUPAGED PLATE

You will need an octagonal clear glass plate (we used a 12" dia. plate), gift wrap, decoupage glue, foam brush, and matte clear acrylic spray sealer.

1. Cut pieces from gift wrap. Use foam brush to apply glue to right side of gift wrap pieces. Working on back of plate and overlapping as desired, glue gift wrap pieces to plate; allow to dry. If necessary, trim excess paper even with edge of plate.
2. Allowing to dry between coats, apply two to three coats of sealer to bottom of plate.
3. Wipe plate with a damp cloth after each use.

STRAWBERRY SWEETHEART CAKES

*O*ur Strawberry *Sweetheart Cakes are delightful tokens of affection for all your valentines! Filled with creamy strawberry icing, the moist, buttery cakes are dusted with confectioners sugar and individually wrapped in cellophane for gift-giving. Handmade tags, pretty ribbons, and faux rosebuds make lovely embellishments for your presents.*

STRAWBERRY SWEETHEART CAKES

Cakes are easier to slice if made ahead and chilled.

CAKES
- 1¹/₂ cups butter or margarine, softened
- 2 cups sugar
- 5 eggs, separated
- 1 tablespoon vanilla extract
- ¹/₂ cup (¹/₂ of an 11¹/₂-ounce jar) strawberry ice cream topping
- 4¹/₂ cups sifted cake flour
- 4¹/₂ teaspoons baking powder
- 1 teaspoon salt
- 1¹/₄ cups milk
- ¹/₄ teaspoon red liquid food coloring

ICING
- ²/₃ cup butter or margarine, softened
- ¹/₂ cup strawberry ice cream topping
- ³/₄ teaspoon vanilla extract
- 7 cups sifted confectioners sugar
- 2 to 3 tablespoons milk
   Confectioners sugar to decorate

Preheat oven to 350 degrees. For cakes, grease each heart-shaped cup of a 6-mold baking pan (each cup is about 3³/₄ inches wide). In a large bowl, cream butter and sugar until fluffy. Add egg yolks and vanilla; beat until smooth. Beat in strawberry topping. In a medium bowl, combine cake flour, baking powder, and salt. Alternately add milk and dry ingredients to creamed mixture; beat until well blended. Tint pink. In a medium bowl, beat egg whites until stiff. Fold into batter. Spoon about ¹/₄ cup batter into each heart-shaped cup. Bake 11 to 13 minutes or until edges are lightly browned and a toothpick inserted in center of cake comes out clean. Cool in pan 5 minutes. Transfer cakes to a wire rack; cool completely. Chill cakes 2 hours before slicing.

For icing, beat butter, strawberry topping, and vanilla in a large bowl until well blended. Gradually add confectioners sugar and 2 tablespoons milk; beating until smooth. Add additional milk to icing, 1 teaspoon at a time, for desired consistency. Slice each cake in half horizontally. Spread about 1 rounded tablespoon icing between layers of each cake. Dust tops with confectioners sugar. Store in a single layer in an airtight container in a cool place.

Yield: about 3 dozen cakes

BIRTHDAY PARTY TREATS

*T*he birthday girl and
her guests will jump for joy
when you present them with
fun favor bags filled with toys,
candy, and our gooey Birthday
Party Treats! The crispy bites
are quickly prepared with
fruit-flavored cereal and
marshmallows. Sure to delight
the partygoers, each goody bag
is tied with curling ribbon and
a jump rope for take-home
fun. A hole-punched tag
personalizes each gift.

BIRTHDAY PARTY TREATS

3/4 teaspoon *each* of the following
    coarse decorating sugars: blue,
    orange, red, violet, green, and
    yellow
  1 package (10 1/2 ounces) miniature
    marshmallows
1/4 cup butter or margarine
 10 cups round fruit-flavored cereal

Line a 9 x 13-inch baking pan with
aluminum foil; grease foil. In a small
bowl, combine decorating sugars; set
aside. In a large Dutch oven, melt
marshmallows and butter over low heat,
stirring frequently. Remove from heat. Stir
in cereal. Use greased hands to press
cereal mixture into prepared pan.
Sprinkle with decorating sugar mixture.
Let cool. Lift from pan using ends of foil.
Cut into 2-inch squares; individually wrap
treats. Store in a cool place.

Yield: about 2 dozen treats

GREAT AMERICAN PIE

Whether fruity, satiny, or chock-full of nuts, pies are one of today's most popular desserts! February is Great American Pie Month — a great time to bake yummy sweets at home. For a taste that's wonderful and unique, make our Creamy Peanut Butter Pie and share it with a pie-loving friend. Attached to a miniature flag, a pen-stitched paper star offers a whimsical salute to a month of delicious pies.

CREAMY PEANUT BUTTER PIE

    1   cup sifted confectioners sugar
   ¹/₂ cup smooth peanut butter
    1   baked 9-inch pie crust
    1   cup plus 3 tablespoons granulated
          sugar, divided
   ¹/₂ cup all-purpose flour
   ¹/₄ teaspoon salt
  2¹/₂ cups milk
   ¹/₂ cup whipping cream
    4   eggs, separated
    1   tablespoon butter or margarine
  1¹/₂ teaspoons vanilla extract
   ¹/₄ teaspoon cream of tartar

In a small bowl, combine confectioners sugar and peanut butter until crumbly. Sprinkle 1 cup of peanut butter mixture over bottom of pie crust; reserve remaining mixture.

In top of a double boiler over simmering water, combine 1 cup granulated sugar, flour, and salt. Whisk in milk, whipping cream, and egg yolks until well blended. Whisking constantly, cook about 20 minutes or until mixture thickens to a pudding consistency. Stir in butter and vanilla. Pour custard over peanut butter mixture.

Preheat oven to 350 degrees. In a medium bowl, beat egg whites and cream of tartar until foamy. Gradually add remaining 3 tablespoons granulated sugar; beat until stiff peaks form. Spread meringue over hot custard sealing edges to crust. Sprinkle reserved peanut butter mixture over meringue. Bake 12 to 16 minutes or until meringue is golden brown. Transfer pie to a wire rack to cool. Store in an airtight container in refrigerator.

Yield: about 8 servings

BIRDHOUSE COOKIES

*P*repare now for the spring return of your feathered friends by fixing up and putting up homes for wild birds. Then reward yourself and the nature-loving friends who help you with gifts of yummy Birdhouse Cookies. Shaped and embellished to resemble birdhouses, the nutty sweets are baked on sticks and displayed in small decorated flowerpots.

BIRDHOUSE COOKIES

COOKIES

- ³/₄ cup butter or margarine, softened
- ¹/₂ cup firmly packed brown sugar
- 1 egg
- 1 teaspoon vanilla extract
- 1²/₃ cups all-purpose flour
- ¹/₂ cup chopped pecans, toasted and coarsely ground
- ¹/₂ teaspoon baking powder
- ¹/₈ teaspoon salt
    Craft sticks

ICING

- 2 cups sifted confectioners sugar
- 2 tablespoons milk
- 2 tablespoons butter or margarine, softened
- 1 teaspoon vanilla extract
    Blue and red paste food coloring
    Stick pretzels

Trace birdhouse pattern, page 110, onto stencil plastic; cut out. For cookies, cream butter and brown sugar in a medium bowl until fluffy. Add egg and vanilla; beat until smooth. In a small bowl, combine flour, pecans, baking

powder, and salt. Add dry ingredients to creamed mixture; stir until a soft dough forms. Divide dough in half. Wrap in plastic wrap and chill 2 hours.

Preheat oven to 350 degrees. On a lightly floured surface, use a floured rolling pin to roll out half of dough to ¹/₄-inch thickness. Place pattern on dough and use a sharp knife to cut out cookies. Place 4 inches apart on a greased baking sheet. Insert a craft stick about 1¹/₄ inches into bottom of each cookie. Cut out a ⁵/₈-inch-diameter circle 1 inch from top of each cookie. Bake 6 to 8 minutes or until edges are lightly browned. Cool

cookies on baking sheet 10 minutes; carefully transfer to a wire rack to cool completely. Repeat with remaining dough.

For icing, combine confectioners sugar, milk, butter, and vanilla in a small bowl; beat until smooth. Divide icing into 2 small bowls; tint blue and red. Spoon icing into pastry bags fitted with small round tips. Outline and fill in each roof with blue icing. Pipe design under roof using red icing. Use blue icing to attach a ³/₄-inch-long pretzel piece to each cookie for "perch." Allow icing to harden. Store in an airtight container in a single layer.

Yield: about 1¹/₂ dozen cookies

22

SPECIAL DELIVERY!

*E*veryone loves a sweet
surprise! Sure to please a secret
pal, this Crunchy Granola
Snack Mix is quick and easy
to toss together, and it's the
perfect treat on a crisp autumn
afternoon. For a special
delivery, "post" a bag of the
mix in a miniature mailbox.

CRUNCHY GRANOLA SNACK MIX

5 cups granola cereal with dried
    fruit and nuts
1 package (10 ounces) candy-
    coated chocolate pieces
1 package (7¹/₂ ounces) French
    burnt candy-coated peanuts
1 cup honey-roasted peanuts
1 cup raisins

Combine cereal, chocolate pieces,
peanuts, and raisins in a large bowl. Store
in an airtight container.

Yield: about 9 cups snack mix

*P*aint a smile on the face of your favorite little Picasso with a gift of edible Artists' Cookie Crayons! A masterpiece of crisp texture and peanut butter flavor, the imaginative treats make a brilliant reminder to live life with creative flair — for example, transforming an empty cake mix box into a crafty cookie container! The easy-to-make holder is simply covered with fabric or wrapping paper and decorated with an inspiring tag.

ARTISTS' COOKIE CRAYONS

COOKIES

1	cup butter or margarine, softened
¹/₂	cup vegetable shortening
1¹/₂	cups granulated sugar
¹/₂	cup firmly packed brown sugar
1	cup smooth peanut butter
2	eggs
1	teaspoon vanilla extract
4	cups all-purpose flour
1¹/₄	cups sweetened corn flake cereal, finely crushed
¹/₄	teaspoon salt

ICING

7¹/₂	cups sifted confectioners sugar
10	to 12 tablespoons milk
	Yellow, blue, red, orange, violet, and green paste food coloring
1	tube (4¹/₄ ounces) chocolate decorating icing

For cookies, cream butter, shortening, and sugars in a large bowl until fluffy. Add peanut butter, eggs, and vanilla; beat until smooth. In a medium bowl, combine flour, crushed cereal, and salt. Add dry ingredients to creamed mixture; stir until a soft dough forms. Divide dough into fourths; wrap each fourth in plastic wrap. Chill 1 hour.

Preheat oven to 350 degrees. On a lightly floured surface, use a floured rolling pin to roll out one fourth dough into a 10-inch square. Cut out 1 x 5-inch cookies. Transfer to a greased baking sheet. Cut 1 end of each cookie to form a point. Bake 8 to 10 minutes or until edges are lightly browned. Cool cookies on baking sheet 2 minutes; transfer to a wire rack to cool completely. Repeat with remaining dough.

For icing, combine confectioners sugar and milk in a medium bowl. Transfer ¹/₂ cup icing into each of 6 small bowls. Tint yellow, blue, red, orange, violet, and green. Spoon icings into pastry bags fitted with small round tips. Outline and fill in "labels" with icing. Allow icing to harden.

Transfer chocolate icing into a pastry bag fitted with a small round tip. Pipe names of colors and lines onto cookies. Allow icing to harden. Store in an airtight container.

Yield: about 6¹/₂ dozen cookies

COOKIE CRAYON BOX

You will need an empty cake mix box (we used a 5¹/₄" x 7¹/₄" box), fabric to cover box, craft knife, spray adhesive, and glue.

For label, you will *also* need yellow and purple paper, tracing paper, transfer paper, decorative-edge craft scissors, and a black permanent felt-tip pen.

1. Use glue to reseal box.

2. Cut a piece from fabric large enough to completely cover box. Apply spray adhesive to wrong side of fabric. Wrapping box like a package, press fabric in place. Glue overlapped edges of fabric in place as necessary.

3. Place box on one side. Use craft knife to cut box lid (Fig. 1).

Fig. 1

1³/₄"

4. For label, trace pattern, page 110, on tracing paper. Use pattern to cut label from yellow paper. Use transfer paper to transfer words to center of label. Use pen to draw over transferred words. Glue label to purple paper. Leaving a ¹/₄" purple border, use craft scissors to cut out label. Glue label to front of box.

IRISH MINTS

*O*n St. Patrick's Day, share our Minty Chocolate Creams with your co-workers so that everyone can have a wee bit of Irish luck! The bite-size candies feature buttery cocoa centers cloaked in mint-flavored chocolate. Just for fun, present the goodies in this delightful fabric-covered Shaker box.

MINTY CHOCOLATE CREAMS

- 1 jar (7 ounces) marshmallow creme
- 2/3 cup butter or margarine, softened
- 1 teaspoon vanilla extract
- 6 cups sifted confectioners sugar
- 6 tablespoons cocoa
- 6 ounces chocolate candy coating, chopped
- 1 1/4 cups mint-flavored chocolate chips

In a large bowl, beat marshmallow creme, butter, and vanilla until well blended. In a medium bowl, sift confectioners sugar and cocoa. Gradually add dry ingredients to marshmallow mixture; stir until well blended. Shape teaspoonfuls of candy into 3/4-inch balls. Place on a baking sheet lined with waxed paper. Chill 1 hour or until firm.

In top of a double boiler, melt candy coating and chocolate chips over hot, not simmering, water. Placing each ball on a fork and holding over saucepan, spoon chocolate over balls. Return to baking sheet lined with waxed paper. Chill 30 minutes or until chocolate hardens. Store in an airtight container in refrigerator.

Yield: about 9 dozen candies

SHAMROCK BOX

You will need a 7" dia. Shaker box with lid, fabric to cover box, paper-backed fusible web, 34 1/2" length of 1/4"w satin ribbon, 6"h shamrock doily, white acrylic paint, paintbrush, and glue.

1. Paint lid of box white; allow to dry.
2. Cut a 12" length from ribbon and tie into a bow. Center and glue remaining ribbon length around lid. Glue doily to top of lid. Glue bow to doily.
3. To cover sides of box, measure height of box; add 1/2". Measure around box; add 1". Cut one piece *each* from fabric and web the determined measurements. Fuse web to wrong side of fabric.
4. Press one end of fabric 1/2" to wrong side. Beginning with unpressed end and matching one long edge to top edge of box, fuse fabric around box. Glue fabric at overlap to secure. At bottom of box, clip fabric at 1/2" intervals to 1/8" from bottom of box. Fuse clipped edges of fabric to bottom of box.
5. To cover bottom of box, draw around bottom of box on paper side of web. Fuse web to wrong side of fabric. Cut out circle 1/8" inside drawn line. Center and fuse fabric shape to bottom of box.

26

ST. PATRICK'S GOLD

Lucky leprechauns will discover that our Pot of Gold Cookies are the real treasure at the end of the rainbow! For sharing, the rich pecan cookies are piled high in a purchased container decorated with a handmade rainbow and gift tag.

POT OF GOLD COOKIES

- ³/₄ cup butter or margarine, softened
- ¹/₂ cup firmly packed brown sugar
- ¹/₂ cup granulated sugar
- 1 egg
- 1 teaspoon vanilla extract
- ¹/₂ teaspoon butter extract
- 1 teaspoon yellow liquid food coloring
- 2 cups all-purpose flour
- ¹/₈ teaspoon salt
- 1 cup chopped pecans, toasted and coarsely ground

Preheat oven to 350 degrees. In a large bowl, cream butter and sugars until fluffy. Add egg, extracts, and food coloring; beat until smooth. In a small bowl, combine flour and salt. Add dry ingredients to creamed mixture; stir until a soft dough forms. Stir in pecans. Shape dough into ³/₄-inch balls and place 2 inches apart on a lightly greased baking sheet. Flatten each ball slightly with fingers to form a 1¹/₂-inch-diameter circle. Bake 5 to 7 minutes or until bottoms are lightly browned. Transfer cookies to a wire rack to cool. Store in an airtight container.

Yield: about 11 dozen cookies

ST. PATRICK'S DAY "POT OF GOLD"

You will need a black bucket with handle (we used a 9" dia. bucket), poster board, colored pencils, 1¹/₂"w green mesh ribbon, 6" length of floral wire, tracing paper, and glue.

For gift tag, you will *also* need a photocopy of tag design (page 119), green paper, and green markers.

1. For rainbow pattern, align one straight edge of tracing paper with edge of work surface. Place rim of bucket against edge of work surface with handle on tracing paper. Draw along handle on tracing paper. Cutting ³/₄" from each side of drawn line, cut out rainbow pattern.

2. Draw around rainbow pattern on poster board; cut out. Use colored pencils to color rainbow; glue to handle.

3. Trace shamrock pattern, page 118, onto tracing paper; cut out. Use pattern to cut three shamrocks from poster board. Use green colored pencil to color shamrocks. Glue to rainbow.

4. Follow *Making a Multi-Loop Bow*, page 122, to make mesh bow. Twist wire ends around handle to secure to pot.

5. For gift tag, use markers to color tag design and write message on tag. Cut out tag.

6. Glue tag to green paper. Leaving a ¹/₄" green border, cut out gift tag.

"Tweet" Spring Treats

An afternoon tea would be a lovely way to welcome spring. For such a special occasion, you'll surely want to serve our pretty Coconut Bird Nests to those in attendance. A trio of jelly bean "eggs" is nestled in each delicate little cookie. Embellished with silk flowers and swirls of wired ribbon, a springtime wreath doubles as a centerpiece and a serving place for a plate of these "tweet" treats.

Coconut Bird Nests

- 1/2 cup butter or margarine, softened
- 3/4 cup sugar
- 1 egg
- 1 teaspoon vanilla extract
- 1/4 teaspoon coconut flavoring
- 1 1/4 cups all-purpose flour
- 1/8 teaspoon salt
- 1 3/4 cups shredded coconut, divided
- 1/2 cup small gourmet jelly beans

In a medium bowl, cream butter and sugar until fluffy. Add egg, vanilla, and coconut flavoring; stir until smooth. In a small bowl, combine flour and salt. Add dry ingredients to creamed mixture; stir until a soft dough forms. Stir in 1/2 cup coconut. Cover and chill 2 1/2 hours or until firm.

Preheat oven to 350 degrees. To toast coconut, place remaining 1 1/4 cups coconut on an ungreased baking sheet. Stirring occasionally, bake 8 to 12 minutes or until coconut is lightly browned; cool. Shape dough into 1-inch

balls. Roll in toasted coconut, pressing coconut into dough. Place 2 inches apart on an ungreased baking sheet. Use thumb to make an indentation in center of each cookie. Press 3 jelly beans into each indentation. In 350-degree oven, bake 8 to 10 minutes or until edges are lightly browned. Transfer cookies to a wire rack to cool completely. Store in an airtight container.

Yield: about 3 dozen cookies

"Welcome Spring!" Gift Tag

You will need a photocopy of tag design (page 119), green paper, black permanent felt-tip pen, colored pencils, decorative-edge craft scissors, and glue.

1. Use pencils to color tag design. Use pen to write message on tag. Cut out tag.
2. Glue tag to green paper. Leaving a 1/4" green border, use craft scissors to cut out gift tag.

GOOFY GOLF BALLS

*I*nternational Goof-Off Day (March 22) encourages relaxation and good-natured silliness. To get your fairway friends in the swing of things, share a batch of Golf Ball Cookies at the 19th hole. Buttery pecan cookies are dipped in creamy vanilla coating for tasty little morsels. A simple wire basket makes a "par-fect" presentation for the treats.

GOLF BALL COOKIES

  2/3 cup butter, softened
    1 cup sifted confectioners sugar
    1 egg
    2 teaspoons vanilla extract
 2¹/₂ cups all-purpose flour
  ¹/₂ cup chopped pecans, toasted and
       coarsely ground
    8 ounces vanilla candy coating,
       chopped
    1 package (6 ounces) white baking
       chocolate, chopped

Preheat oven to 350 degrees. In a large bowl, cream butter and confectioners sugar until fluffy. Add egg and vanilla; beat until smooth. Add flour to creamed mixture; stir until a soft dough forms. Stir in pecans. Shape dough into 1-inch balls and place on a greased baking sheet. Bake 10 to 12 minutes or until bottoms are lightly browned. Transfer cookies to a wire rack to cool.

Melt candy coating and baking chocolate in top of a double boiler over hot, not simmering, water. Remove from heat. Dip cookies into chocolate mixture. Transfer to a baking sheet lined with waxed paper. Chill cookies about 30 minutes or until coating hardens. Store in an airtight container in a cool place.

Yield: about 4¹/₂ dozen cookies

GOOF-OFF DAY FLAG

You will need tracing paper, red paper, black permanent felt-tip pen, bamboo skewer, and glue.

Trace flag pattern, page 111, onto tracing paper; cut out. Use pattern to cut flag from red paper. Use pen to write message on flag. Refer to grey line on pattern to fold tab to back of flag. Glue one end of skewer into fold.

STRAW HAT COOKIES

*T*he old adage that good things come in small packages is especially true when you share our delicate Straw Hat Cookies. Nestled in tiny papier-mâché boxes, the pretty sweets are made by sandwiching purchased cookies together, then adding an icing hatband, a spray of silk flowers, and a satin ribbon bow. The lovely springtime containers are topped with napkin-covered lids and tied with a trio of matching ribbons.

STRAW HAT COOKIES

$3/4$ cup sifted confectioners sugar
$1^1/2$ tablespoons butter or
        margarine, softened
$1^1/4$ teaspoons milk
$1/4$ teaspoon vanilla extract
        Pink paste food coloring
18 scalloped-edge sugar cookies
        (about $2^3/4$ inches in diameter)
18 coconut macaroons (about
        2 inches in diameter)
        Narrow satin ribbon and artificial
        flowers to decorate

In a small bowl, combine confectioners sugar, butter, milk, and vanilla; beat until smooth. Tint icing pink. Spoon icing into a pastry bag fitted with a small petal tip. To decorate each "hat," place 1 sugar cookie bottom side up. Pipe icing onto bottom of 1 macaroon and place in center of sugar cookie. Pipe a "hatband" around bottom of macaroon. Use a small amount of icing to attach a ribbon bow to hatband of each cookie. Use icing to attach flowers to hat. Let icing harden. Store in a single layer in an airtight container.

Yield: 18 hat cookies

SHAKER HAT BOXES

For each box, you will need a $3^3/4$" dia. papier-mâché box with lid; printed paper napkin; $3/4$ yd each of $1/4$"w, $3/16$"w, and $1/8$"w ribbon; white spray paint; and spray adhesive.

1. Spray paint box white; allow to dry.

2. Unfold and press napkin. Separate napkin into layers.

3. Using printed layer of napkin only, place lid of box on wrong side of napkin. Draw around lid. Cutting 1" outside drawn line, cut circle from napkin. Pleating napkin along side of lid as necessary, use spray adhesive to carefully glue napkin circle to top and side of lid; trim excess napkin even with bottom edge of lid.

4. Place cookie in box. Place lid on box. Tie ribbon lengths into a bow around box.

CELEBRATION BAKLAVA

*D*renched in a mixture of honey and liqueur, our Grand Marnier Baklava is well worth a celebration in its own right. However, if you must have a reason to indulge in the flaky, nut-filled pastry, what better occasion than Greek Independence Day (March 25)! For sharing, arrange the baklava on a decorated serving tray and top one piece with a Greek-inspired tag to announce the special day.

GRAND MARNIER BAKLAVA

   3 cups finely chopped walnuts
   1 cup granulated sugar, divided
 ¹/₄ cup firmly packed brown sugar
   1 teaspoon ground cinnamon
   1 package (16 ounces) frozen
         phyllo pastry, thawed
1¹/₄ cups butter, melted
 ³/₄ cup water
 ³/₄ cup honey
 ¹/₄ cup Grand Marnier (orange-
         flavored liqueur)
   2 teaspoons freshly squeezed lemon
         juice

Preheat oven to 325 degrees. In a small bowl, combine walnuts, ¹/₄ cup granulated sugar, brown sugar, and cinnamon.

Unfold phyllo pastry on a flat surface. Cut 1 inch from long side of pastry. Cut pastry in half crosswise (sheets will measure about 8¹/₂ x 12 inches). Brush each of 15 pastry sheets with melted butter; place in a greased 9 x 13-inch baking pan. Cover remaining pastry with a damp cloth. Spoon 2 cups nut mixture

over pastry in pan. Brush 15 additional pastry sheets with butter and place in pan. Spoon remaining nut mixture over pastry. Brush remaining pastry sheets with butter and place in pan. Use a very sharp knife to score top layer of pastry sheets into 2-inch squares. Bake 45 to 55 minutes or until golden brown. Cool in pan on a wire rack.

In a medium saucepan, combine remaining ³/₄ cup granulated sugar, water, and honey over medium-high heat. Stirring constantly, bring syrup to a boil. Reduce heat to medium-low. Stirring occasionally, simmer 10 minutes. Remove from heat. Stir in liqueur and lemon juice. Slowly pour warm syrup over baklava. Allow to cool 4 hours at room temperature. Cut into squares. Store in an airtight container.

Yield: about 24 servings

GREEK SERVING TRAY

You will need a 15" dia. galvanized tray, iridescent acrylic jewels (we used 17mm jewels), and silver dimensional paint. *For tag*, you will *also* need white poster board, blue felt-tip marker, black permanent felt-tip pen, bamboo skewer, and glue.

1. Use dimensional paint to paint designs on rim of tray.
2. To attach each jewel, squeeze a dot of paint on rim of tray same size as jewel. While paint is still wet, press jewel into paint; allow to dry.
3. For tag, cut a 2¹/₈" x 3³/₈" piece from poster board. Use marker to color flag design on poster board piece. Use pen to write message on tag.
4. Cut a 6" length from skewer. Leaving bottom 1¹/₈" of skewer uncolored, use marker to color skewer blue. Glue top of skewer to back of flag.
5. Wipe tray with a damp cloth after each use.

Gardens not only contribute to the beauty of the land, but they're also responsible for lots of good things to eat! Encourage a friend to "preserve" the fruits of her labor with this pretty gift basket containing Orange-Fig Preserves, decorated gardening gloves, and a ready-to-use flowerpot. The handy gloves are accented with eyelet lace and fused-on fabric motifs. Decorated with a raffia bow and glued-on fabric pieces, the rustic basket is just the right size for displaying a windowsill garden.

ORANGE-FIG PRESERVES

   2 packages (8 ounces each) dried figs, chopped (we used Calimyrna figs)
   2 cups water
 ²/₃ cup sugar
   1 cup orange marmalade

In a heavy medium saucepan, combine figs, water, and sugar. Stirring frequently, bring mixture to a boil over medium-high heat. Reduce heat to medium-low and simmer uncovered 20 minutes or until figs are tender. Stir in marmalade. Stirring frequently, cook 10 minutes longer. Spoon preserves into heat-resistant jars; cover and cool to room temperature. Store in refrigerator.

Yield: about 4 cups preserves

"KEEP AMERICA BEAUTIFUL" BASKET

You will need a basket with handle (we used a 3³/₄" x 9" basket), fruit-motif fabric, two 2" x 2¹/₂" torn fabric pieces, paper-backed fusible web, a pair of cotton gardening gloves, 19" length of lace trim, 3⁵/₈"h flowerpot, green excelsior, green raffia, and glue.
For tag, you will *also* need a 2" x 3¹/₄" handmade paper piece, 6³/₄" long twig, and a black permanent felt-tip pen.

1. Fuse web to wrong side of fruit-motif fabric. Cut desired motifs for gloves and basket from fabric.
2. Fuse one motif to each glove.
3. Cut trim in half. Glue one trim length around bottom of each cuff.
4. Fuse remaining motif to one fabric piece. Overlap and glue fabric pieces to basket.
5. For tag, cut jagged edges along each short side of paper piece. Use pen to write message on tag. Glue paper piece to top of twig.
6. Place excelsior in flowerpot and basket. Place preserves and tag in flowerpot. Place flowerpot and gloves in basket.
7. Tie several lengths of raffia into a bow around basket handle.

ORANGE-FIG PRESERVES

Keep America
Beautiful...
Preserve

APRIL FOOLS' CANDY

*T*he big surprise in
our whimsical April Fools'
Candy is not just the sassy
jalapeño flavor; it's also
the fact that the chewy little
bites are truly delicious!
Piped-on icing peppers offer
a hint to the nature of the
fiery squares, which are
packed in purchased candy
boxes. We cut letters from
magazines and glued them
in the boxes to spell out the
mischievous message.

APRIL FOOLS' CANDY

- 1 cup sugar
- 1 cup light corn syrup
- 1 to 2 jalapeño peppers, seeded and finely chopped
- 3/4 cup water
- 1 package (1 3/4 ounces) powdered fruit pectin
- 1/2 teaspoon baking soda
- 3 drops green liquid food coloring
- 8 ounces vanilla candy coating, chopped
- 4 ounces white baking chocolate Red and green oil-based candy coloring

Line a 5 x 9-inch loaf pan with aluminum foil, extending foil over ends of pan; grease foil. Butter sides of a heavy medium saucepan. Combine sugar, corn syrup, and jalapeño pepper. Stirring constantly, cook over medium-low heat until sugar dissolves. Using a pastry brush dipped in hot water, wash down any sugar crystals on sides of pan. Attach a candy thermometer to pan, making sure

thermometer does not touch bottom of pan. Increase heat to medium-high and bring to a boil. While cooking sugar mixture, combine water, pectin, and baking soda in another medium saucepan. Stirring frequently, cook pectin mixture over high heat until mixture boils. Remove from heat. Cook sugar mixture, stirring occasionally, until mixture reaches soft-crack stage (approximately 270 to 290 degrees). Test about 1/2 teaspoon mixture in ice water. Mixture will form hard threads in ice water but will soften when removed from the water. Bring pectin mixture back to a boil. Stirring constantly, slowly pour sugar mixture into boiling pectin mixture; cook 2 minutes. Remove from heat. Stir in green food coloring. Pour mixture into prepared pan. Allow mixture to cool 2 hours or until firm.

Lift candy from pan using edges of foil. Use a greased knife to cut into 3/4 x 1-inch pieces. In a heavy medium saucepan over low heat, melt candy coating and white chocolate. Remove chocolate mixture from heat (if mixture begins to harden, return to heat). Placing each jelly candy on a fork and holding over saucepan, spoon chocolate mixture over candy. Place candies on a baking sheet covered with waxed paper; chill 10 minutes.

Divide remaining white chocolate mixture in half into 2 small bowls. Tint red and green. Spoon each color into a pastry bag fitted with a small round tip. Pipe red mixture onto each candy for "pepper." Pipe green mixture onto each pepper for "stem." Allow decorations to harden. Store in an airtight container in a cool place.

Yield: about 4 dozen candies

RACE-DAY GOODIES

*H*ere's a speedy gift that's sure to get the checkered flag from racing fans! Our man-size popcorn bowl is decoupaged with colorful labels and piled high with race-day goodies, including car magazines, a TV program guide, and lots of microwave popcorn for munching. To add zip to the taste of this natural snack, we also tucked in a jar of Spicy Popcorn Seasoning — it's a zesty blend of high-octane flavors! A photocopied tag is tied to the jar for a fast finish.

SPICY POPCORN SEASONING

> 3 tablespoons dried parsley flakes
> 2¹/₂ tablespoons chili powder
> 2 tablespoons garlic salt
> 1 tablespoon dried chives
> 2 teaspoons onion powder

Combine all ingredients in a small bowl. Store in an airtight container. Give with serving instructions.

Yield: about ¹/₂ cup seasoning mix

To serve: Combine ¹/₃ cup butter or margarine and 1 tablespoon seasoning mix in a small microwave-safe bowl. Cover and microwave on medium power (50%) 1 minute or until butter melts. Drizzle over 15 cups popped popcorn; toss to coat popcorn.

DECOUPAGED BOWL

You will need an acrylic bowl (we used a 5¹/₂"h x 11" dia. bowl), fabric for bowl liner, labels removed from assorted beverage bottles, foam brush, decoupage glue, and clear acrylic spray sealer.
For tag, you will *also* need a photocopy of tag design (page 119), red permanent felt-tip pen, poster board, 4"l bamboo skewer, and glue.

1. Use foam brush to apply decoupage glue to wrong side of each label. Glue labels to outside of bowl, overlapping labels as desired; allow to dry.

2. Place bowl upside down on a flat surface. Allowing to dry between coats, apply two to three coats of sealer to outside of bowl.
3. Follow *Making a Basket Liner*, page 124, to make liner with an unfinished edge for bowl. Place liner in bowl.
4. For tag, use pen to write message on tag. Glue tag to poster board; cut out. Glue skewer to back of tag.
5. Lightly hand wash inside of bowl after each use.

35

EARTH DAY ENERGIZER SNACK

A day set aside to reclaim the purity of the environment, Earth Day (April 22) is the ideal time to enjoy a picnic and nature walk. Our crunchy Earth Day Snack Mix is an energy-boosting treat to munch along the trail. It's packaged in a clever "recycled" gift container that's sure to please Mother Nature.

EARTH DAY SNACK MIX

- 2 cups small pretzel twists
- 2 cups round toasted oat cereal
- 2 cups square rice cereal
- 2 cups fruit-flavored corn puff cereal
- 2 cups sweetened wheat puff cereal
- 2 cups toasted plain croutons
- 2 cups cheese snack crackers
- 2 cups rippled cheese cracker chips
- 2 cups assorted nuts
- 1/2 cup butter or margarine
- 1 cup firmly packed brown sugar
- 1/4 cup light corn syrup
- 1/2 teaspoon salt
- 1/2 teaspoon vanilla extract
- 1/2 teaspoon baking soda
- 1 cup raisins

Preheat oven to 275 degrees. In a large roasting pan, combine pretzels, cereals, croutons, crackers, chips, and nuts. In a heavy medium saucepan, combine butter, brown sugar, corn syrup, and salt over medium heat. Stirring constantly, bring to a boil; boil 5 minutes without stirring. Remove from heat. Stir in vanilla and baking soda. Pour mixture over dry ingredients; stir until well coated. Bake 1 hour, stirring every 15 minutes and adding raisins after 30 minutes. Spread on greased aluminum foil to cool. Store in an airtight container.

Yield: about 22 cups snack mix

EARTH DAY GIFT CONTAINER

You will need a two-liter plastic beverage bottle with cap, 2/3 yd each of 3/8"w green and 3/8"w blue ribbon, green and blue acrylic paint, sponge pieces, paintbrush, four pop-tops from aluminum beverage cans, bubble wrap, small brown paper grocery bag, black permanent felt-tip marker, compass, serrated-edge craft scissors, craft knife, clear packing tape, and glue.

1. Use craft knife to cut a 6" long vertical slit in back of bottle. Place snack mix in bottle through slit. Cut an 8" length of packing tape. Fold one end 1/2" to adhesive side. Use tape to seal slit in bottle.

2. For label, use craft scissors to cut a 6" x 15" piece from bag. Use compass to draw a 4 1/2" dia. circle at center of paper piece. Paint circle blue; allow to dry. Use sponge pieces and follow *Sponge Painting,* page 123, to paint green continents on circle. Use marker to write "EARTH DAY" around circle. Glue label around bottle.

3. Cut a 2" x 17" strip from bubble wrap. Tie bubble wrap strip into a bow. Knot ribbon lengths around neck of bottle and tie into a bow around bubble wrap bow. Thread pop-tops onto ends of ribbons; glue to secure.

RED-HOT ANNIVERSARY BASKET

*H*ere's a red-hot gift
for a couple whose romance
still sizzles years after the
honeymoon! Snappy
Strawberry-Jalapeño Sauce
is wonderfully spicy and sweet
— sort of like the deserving
couple. For their immediate
enjoyment, the sauce is placed
in a charming anniversary
basket along with crackers
and a tangy Cheddar-cream
cheese blend.

SNAPPY STRAWBERRY-JALAPEÑO SAUCE

  2 jars (18 ounces each) strawberry
      preserves
  1 jar (12 ounces) pickled jalapeño
      pepper slices, drained

Pulse process preserves and jalapeño
slices in a food processor until peppers
are finely chopped. Pour into 4 half-pint
jars; cover and store in refrigerator. Give
with serving instructions.

Yield: about 4 cups sauce

To serve: In a medium bowl, combine
8 ounces softened cream cheese and
8 ounces finely shredded sharp Cheddar
cheese; beat until well blended. Spread
into a serving dish. Spoon 1 cup sauce
over cheese. Serve with crackers.

ANNIVERSARY BASKET

You will need a basket with handle (we
used a 7¹/₂" x 13¹/₂" basket), fabric for
basket liner, 1¹/₄"w ribbon, jute twine,
and an artificial strawberry stem with
blossoms and leaves.
For gift tag, you will *also* need white
paper, red paper, blue permanent felt-tip
pen, hole punch, and glue.

1. Follow *Making a Basket Liner,*
page 124, to make liner with an
unfinished edge. Place liner in basket.
2. Follow *Making a Multi-Loop Bow,*
page 122, to make one bow *each* from
ribbon and twine.

3. Tie a length of twine around strawberry
stem; tie ends of twine around center
of bows. Tie stem and bows to basket
handle.
4. For gift tag, cut a 1¹/₂" x 3¹/₂" piece
from white paper. Use pen to write
message on paper piece. Glue paper piece
to red paper. Leaving a ³/₈" red border,
cut out gift tag.
5. Punch hole in corner of tag. Cut a 6"
length of twine. Thread twine through
hole and tie tag to basket handle.

EASTER BUNNY TREATS

*D*eliver Easter Bunny *Treats as a fun gift the whole family can enjoy! A colorful combination of assorted holiday candies is packed in a plain glass cookie jar that's embellished with a hand-painted label and a festive bow. The whimsical jar will be a wonderful reminder of your thoughtfulness long after the treats are gone.*

EASTER BUNNY TREATS

16 cups Easter candies (we used malted milk robin eggs, foil-wrapped chocolate eggs, animal-shaped tangy candies, and bunny-shaped marshmallows)

Combine Easter candies in a large bowl. Place candies in gift container.

Yield: 16 cups candy

BUNNY TREATS JAR

You will need a large clear glass cookie jar with smooth, straight sides and a lid with a knob (we used a 7" dia. jar); ²/₃ yd of 1¹/₂"w wired ribbon; white, orange, green, and purple Liquitex® Glossies™ acrylic enamel paint; small paintbrushes; black permanent felt-tip pen; tracing paper; and removable tape.

Refer to Painting Techniques, page 123, for painting tips.

1. Trace pattern, page 111, onto tracing paper. Tape pattern to inside of jar.
2. Painting on outside of jar, paint letters purple, carrots orange, and leaves green. Paint background of design white; allow to dry.
3. Remove pattern.
4. Use pen to draw around and add detail lines to letters, carrots, and leaves.
5. Tie ribbon into a bow around knob on lid.

EASTER SURPRISE

*D*renched in a citrusy chocolate coating, Orange-Mocha Coffee Beans are gourmet candies for adult taste buds. For an Easter delivery that's really hopping, present your gift in a miniature carrot-shaped cart and add a handmade tag.

ORANGE-MOCHA COFFEE BEANS

- 3 tablespoons chocolate-flavored coffee beans
- 1 package (6 ounces) semisweet chocolate chips
- 4 ounces chocolate candy coating
- 1/2 teaspoon finely grated orange zest
- 2 drops orange-flavored oil (used in candy making)

Place coffee beans about 1 inch apart on a baking sheet covered with waxed paper. In top of a double boiler, combine chocolate chips, candy coating, orange zest, and oil. Stirring constantly, cook over hot, not simmering, water until mixture is smooth. Remove from heat. Spoon about 1/4 teaspoon chocolate mixture over each coffee bean. Chill 1 hour or until chocolate hardens. Store in an airtight container in a cool place.

Yield: about 11 dozen candies

"HAPPY EASTER!" GIFT TAG

You will need a photocopy of tag design (page 119), green paper, purple and green markers, decorative-edge craft scissors, and glue.

1. Use green marker to color tag design. Use purple marker to write message on tag. Cut out tag.

2. Glue tag to green paper. Leaving a 1/4" green border, use craft scissors to cut out gift tag.

With today's trend toward simpler meals, the once-nondescript salad has become the stuff that meals are made of — or at the very least, they're refreshing alternatives to heavy side dishes. Our flavorful Salmon Pasta Salad stirs in fresh dill, vegetables, and a dash of lemon juice. The chilled salad is ideal for taking to a spring supper, and an easy-to-paint glass bowl makes a pretty keepsake for the hostess.

SALMON PASTA SALAD

1⅓ cups mayonnaise
1 cup finely chopped green onions
⅔ cup finely chopped celery
¼ cup chopped fresh dill weed
2 tablespoons freshly squeezed lemon juice
2 teaspoons prepared mustard
½ teaspoon ground black pepper
1 package (12 ounces) seashell pasta, cooked
4 packages (3 ounces each) smoked salmon, cut into pieces
Fresh dill weed sprigs to garnish

In a large bowl, combine mayonnaise, green onions, celery, dill weed, lemon juice, mustard, and pepper; stir until well blended. Add pasta; stir until well coated. Stir in salmon. Cover and chill 2 hours to let flavors blend. Garnish with dill weed.

Yield: about 9½ cups salad

PAINTED SALAD BOWL

You will need a 9" dia. glass salad bowl with smooth sides; yellow, red, and green Delta CeramDecor™ Air-Dry Perm Enamel™ paint; paintbrushes; tracing paper; and removable tape.

Refer to Painting Techniques, page 123, for painting tips.

1. Trace leaves and swirl patterns, page 111, separately on tracing paper. Leaving a ½" border around each design, cut out.
2. Tape patterns to inside of bowl.
3. Painting on outside of bowl only, use green paint to paint leaves on bowl; highlight with yellow paint. Use red paint to paint swirl design. Use wrong end of paintbrush to paint yellow and red dots.
4. Repeat Steps 2 and 3, moving patterns for desired placement of design.
5. Remove patterns.
6. Hand wash bowl after each use.

SALMON PASTA SALAD

FLOWER BASKET CAKE

Celebrate the newness of spring by hosting an afternoon tea. Our lovely Springtime Cake would make a magnificent dessert for May Day — or any day! The zesty lemon cake is wrapped in a basket weave of tangy icing and crowned with a bouquet of pretty, edible posies. A simple paper twist handle and wired-ribbon bows are added for a sweet finish.

SPRINGTIME CAKE

CAKE

- 1/2 cup butter or margarine, softened
- 1 1/2 cups sugar
- 3 eggs, separated
- 1/4 cup freshly squeezed lemon juice
- 1 tablespoon grated lemon zest
- 2 1/4 cups all-purpose flour
- 2 teaspoons baking powder
- 1/2 teaspoon salt
- 1 cup milk

ICING

- 6 cups sifted confectioners sugar
- 3/4 cup vegetable shortening
- 3/4 cup butter or margarine, softened
- 3 to 4 tablespoons milk
- 1 teaspoon vanilla extract
- 1 teaspoon lemon extract
  Brown, green, rose, violet, and yellow paste food coloring

Preheat oven to 325 degrees. Heavily grease a 2 1/2-quart ovenproof glass bowl with shortening and dust with flour; set aside.

For cake, cream butter and sugar in a large bowl until fluffy. Add egg yolks, lemon juice, and lemon zest; beat until smooth. In a medium bowl, combine flour, baking powder, and salt. Alternately add milk and dry ingredients to creamed mixture; beat until well blended. In a medium bowl, beat egg whites until stiff; fold into batter. Pour batter into prepared bowl. Bake 1 hour to 1 hour 20 minutes or until a toothpick inserted in center of cake comes out clean. Cool in bowl 10 minutes. Invert cake onto a wire rack to cool completely.

For icing, combine confectioners sugar, shortening, butter, milk, and extracts in a large bowl; beat until smooth. Divide icing into 6 small bowls and tint as follows: 2 cups light brown, 1 1/2 cups light green, 1/2 cup rose, 1/2 cup violet, 1/4 cup medium green, and 1/4 cup yellow. Place cake, wide end up, on a serving plate. Spread light green icing on top. Spoon brown icing into a pastry bag fitted with a basket weave tip. With serrated side of tip up, pipe a vertical stripe of frosting from bottom to top edge of cake. Pipe four 1-inch-long horizontal stripes over vertical stripe about 1 tip width apart (Fig. 1).

Fig. 1

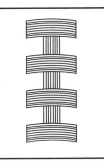

Overlapping ends of horizontal stripes, pipe another vertical stripe to the right of the first vertical stripe (Fig. 2a). Pipe three 1-inch-long horizontal stripes as shown in Fig. 2b.

Fig. 2a

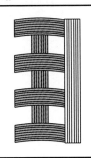

Fig. 2b

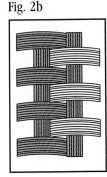

Repeat basket weave design until sides of cake are covered. Use a large star tip to pipe decorative border along bottom and top edges of cake. Use a small rose petal tip and rose and violet icing to pipe 5-petal flowers onto top of cake. Use a small round tip and yellow icing to pipe flower centers. Use a leaf tip and medium green icing to pipe leaves. Cover and store in refrigerator.

Yield: about 14 servings

CAKE HANDLE

You will need 2 1/2 yds of brown paper twist, two 21" lengths of 1 1/2"w wired ribbon, two 6" lengths of floral wire, and two toothpicks.

Cut paper twist into three equal lengths. Place three ends together. Wrap one wire length around ends; twist to secure. Braid paper twist lengths together. Wrap remaining wire length around opposite ends; twist to secure. Tie one ribbon length into a bow around each end, covering wire. Use toothpicks to attach handle to cake.

FIESTA PUNCH

*B*ursting with sunny
flavors, this breezy drink mixer
will wake up the taste buds on
Cinco de Mayo (May 5)! This
Mexican holiday provides a
great time to get together with
friends and sip tangy Fiesta
Punch. The fruity beverage is
equally refreshing whether
served with or without alcohol.
Lined with brightly hued
paper, our party basket
includes painted glasses to
ensure that your gift has
the spirit of a real festival!

FIESTA PUNCH MIX

  1 bottle (33.8 ounces) margarita mix
  1 can (6 ounces) frozen
       orange juice concentrate, thawed
  ¹/₂ cup freshly squeezed lime juice
      Lime and orange slices

In a large container, combine margarita
mix, orange juice, and lime juice. Cover
and store in refrigerator. Add fruit slices
and give with serving instructions.

Yield: about 5³/₄ cups punch mix

To serve: For punch, combine entire
recipe of punch mix with 6 cups chilled
lemon-lime soft drink. Serve chilled.

For a variation, combine entire recipe
of punch mix with 8 ounces tequila and a
dash of salt. Serve over ice.

44

CINCO DE MAYO BASKET

You will need a basket (we used a
13" dia. basket); plastic stemmed goblets
(we used goblets with 3¹/₄" dia. bases);
yellow, orange, red, green, and purple
DecoArt™ Ultra™ Gloss acrylic enamel
paint; paintbrushes; tracing paper;
removable tape; tissue paper; yellow and
green shredded paper; and glue.
For tag, you will *also* need orange paper
and red and black permanent felt-tip
pens.

*Refer to Painting Techniques, page 123,
for painting tips.*

1. Trace sun A and sun B patterns,
page 112, on tracing paper; cut out.

2. For each goblet, use tape to secure
sun A pattern to inside of goblet. Painting
on outside of goblet, paint sun as desired.
Tape sun B pattern to bottom of goblet
base. Painting on top of base, paint sun
as desired.
3. Remove patterns.
4. For tag, trace around outside line of
sun B pattern on orange paper; cut out.
Use red pen to draw lines along edges
of tag. Use black pen to write message
on tag.
5. Place tissue paper and shredded paper
in basket. Glue tag to tissue paper.

HEARTY HERB BREAD

Fragrant herbs have long been prized for their flavorful contribution to many of our favorite foods. In recognition of National Herb Week (the first full week of May), we created golden Casserole Herb Bread. The tasty loaf, which features fresh thyme, oregano, and sage, is presented in a beribboned basket.

CASSEROLE HERB BREAD

1 package dry yeast
1/4 cup warm water
1 cup small-curd cottage cheese
1 tablespoon sugar
1 tablespoon butter, melted
1 teaspoon salt
1/4 teaspoon baking soda
1 egg
1 teaspoon *each* of the following chopped fresh herbs: thyme, oregano, and sage leaves
2 1/4 cups all-purpose flour, divided
  Vegetable cooking spray
1 egg
1 tablespoon milk
  Fresh sage leaves to garnish

In a small bowl, combine yeast and warm water. In a large bowl, combine cottage cheese, sugar, melted butter, salt, baking soda, and 1 egg; beat until blended. Add herbs, yeast mixture, and 1 1/4 cups flour; beat until well blended. Stir in remaining 1 cup flour. Cover and let rise in a warm place (80 to 85 degrees) 1 1/2 hours or until doubled in size.

Turn dough onto a lightly floured surface and punch down. Shape dough into a ball and place in a greased 1 1/2-quart round baking dish. Spray top of dough with cooking spray. Cover and let rise 40 minutes or until almost doubled in size.

Preheat oven to 325 degrees. In a small bowl, beat 1 egg and milk until blended. Brush egg wash over dough. Garnish with fresh sage leaves; brush sage leaves with egg wash. Bake 30 to 35 minutes or until firm and golden brown; cover with aluminum foil during last 10 to 15 minutes if top browns too quickly. Cool in baking dish 20 minutes. Serve warm or transfer to a wire rack to cool completely. Store in an airtight container.

Yield: 1 loaf bread

HERB WEEK GIFT TAG

You will need a photocopy of tag design (page 119), tan paper, brown and green colored pencils, brown marker, serrated-edge craft scissors, hole punch, raffia, and glue.

1. Using supplies for gift tag, follow *Making a Tag*, page 122, to make gift tag.
2. Punch hole in tag. Use a piece of raffia to tie tag to gift.

ROSES FOR MOM

*T*his year, delight Mom with a beautiful rose that's edible, too! Artfully shaped into a lovely blossom, our Rosewater Spread blends the delicate flavor of rose water with sweetened cream cheese. For a sentimental Mother's Day presentation, offer the spread in a pretty teacup with a matching saucer and spreader.

ROSEWATER SPREAD

¹/₃ cup butter, softened
 1 package (3 ounces) cream cheese, softened
 2 tablespoons rose water (available at gourmet food stores)
 1 drop red liquid food coloring
3¹/₂ cups sifted confectioners sugar
   Plain sweet wafer cookies

In a medium bowl, combine butter, cream cheese, rose water, and food coloring; beat until fluffy. Add confectioners sugar; beat until smooth. Spoon into a serving container. Chill 30 minutes or until firm enough to shape. Use a small, warm, dry metal spatula to shape a rose design in spread (warm spatula in hot water and wipe dry). Store in an airtight container in refrigerator. Serve at room temperature with cookies.

Yield: about 2¹/₄ cups spread

MOTHER'S DAY GIFT TAG

You will need a photocopy of tag design (page 119), pink paper, green and pink markers, black calligraphy pen, decorative-edge craft scissors, 25" length each of 1¹/₂"w sheer pink and white ribbons, hole punch, and glue.

1. Use markers to color tag design. Use pen to write message on tag. Cut out tag.
2. Glue tag to pink paper. Leaving a ¹/₄" pink border, use craft scissors to cut out gift tag.
3. Punch hole in corner of tag. Thread ribbons through hole and tie to gift.

HAT BOX CHEESECAKES

*H*ats off to moms the world over! As a unique remembrance, present your mother with a pretty fabric-covered "hat" box filled with delectable Mini Chocolate-Mint Cheesecakes. The bite-size cakes have sweet cookie-crumb crusts and creamy mint filling. The dainty container, crafted from a papier-mâché Shaker box and cardboard, doubles as a trinket holder once the treats are gone.

MINI CHOCOLATE-MINT CHEESECAKES

- 1/2 cup plus 4 teaspoons chocolate sandwich cookie crumbs
- 1 package (10 ounces) individually wrapped layered chocolate mints
- 2 packages (8 ounces each) cream cheese, softened
- 1/2 cup sugar
- 2 eggs
- 1 teaspoon vanilla extract

Line a miniature muffin pan with paper muffin cups. Press about 1/2 teaspoon cookie crumbs into bottom of each paper-lined tin; set aside.

Preheat oven to 350 degrees. In a medium microwave-safe bowl, melt chocolate mints on medium power (50%) 2 minutes, stirring every 30 seconds. Cool to room temperature.

In a large bowl, combine cream cheese and sugar; beat until fluffy. Add eggs and vanilla; beat until well blended. Stir in melted chocolate. Spoon 1 tablespoon mixture over each crust. Bake 24 to 28 minutes or until tops of cheesecakes are cracked and appear dry. Place pan on a wire rack to cool. Store in refrigerator in an airtight container.

Yield: about 4 dozen mini cheesecakes

MOTHER'S DAY HAT

You will need a 6" dia. x 2½"h papier-mâché Shaker box with lid, fabric, 1 yd of 2¼"w white grosgrain ribbon, 20" length *each* of ⅝"w and 1½"w ribbon, 38¾" length of ½"w lace trim, paper-backed fusible web, 12" dia. cardboard cake circle, two artificial daisies with leaves, and glue.

1. For hat crown, remove lid from box. Draw around lid on paper side of web. Cut out circle along drawn line. Fuse circle to wrong side of fabric. Cut out fabric ½" outside edge of web. Clip circle at ½" intervals to ⅛" from web. Center and fuse circle to lid; glue clipped edges to side of lid.

2. For ribbon trim, glue ⅝"w ribbon around side of lid. Cut a 20" length of 2¼"w ribbon and glue around box. Glue 1½"w ribbon around box.

3. For hat brim, draw around cake circle on paper side of web. Fuse web to wrong side of fabric. Cut out along drawn line. Fuse fabric to cake circle.

4. Center and glue hat crown to hat brim. Glue lace trim along edge of brim.

5. Tie remaining ribbon length into a bow and glue to side of box. Glue daisies to knot of bow.

SLEEPY TEA MIX

*I*ndulge a favorite night-owl with our sugar-free Lemon-Raspberry Sleepy Tea Mix — it's a great way to remind her of the benefits of a good night's sleep! To lull your friend into peaceful slumber, encourage her to sip a cup of the fruity decaffeinated tea before bedtime. Sweet dreams!

LEMON-RASPBERRY SLEEPY TEA MIX

1 cup decaffeinated lemon-flavored artificially sweetened powdered instant tea mix
1 package (0.3 ounce) sugar-free raspberry gelatin

Combine tea mix and gelatin in a resealable plastic bag. Give with serving instructions.

Yield: about 1 cup tea mix

To serve: Pour 6 ounces hot water over 1 to 2 teaspoons tea mix; stir until well blended.

"SWEET DREAMS!" GIFT TAG

You will need poster board, tracing paper, transfer paper, colored pencils, and a black permanent felt-tip pen.

1. Trace tag pattern, page 120, on tracing paper. Draw around pattern on poster board. Cut out tag along drawn line.

2. Use transfer paper to transfer words to tag. Use colored pencils to color tag and to draw over transferred words. Use pen to add detail lines along edges of tag as desired.

IT'S GRILLING SEASON!

*T*he sunny days of May provide lots of time for one of our favorite warm weather activities — cookouts! As a great gift for the "grill master," present our Italian Cracked Pepper Seasoning along with a couple of handy new cooking utensils. The aromatic seasoning blend imparts a deliciously piquant flavor to baked or grilled meats. A clever "matchbook" package for the seasoning is easy to construct from fabric-covered poster board.

ITALIAN CRACKED PEPPER SEASONING

- 1/2 cup cracked black pepper
- 1 teaspoon dried basil leaves
- 1 teaspoon dried thyme leaves
- 1 teaspoon dried oregano leaves
- 1 teaspoon dried sage leaves
- 1/2 teaspoon dried rosemary leaves

Combine all ingredients in a resealable plastic bag. Use to season meats before baking or grilling.

Yield: about 1/2 cup seasoning

FABRIC-COVERED PACKAGE

You will need white poster board, two coordinating fabrics, paper-backed fusible web, natural raffia, and desired barbecue tools.

For gift tag, you will *also* need photocopy of tag design (page 119), yellow paper, black permanent felt-tip pen, colored pencils, decorative-edge craft scissors, and glue.

1. Cut one 5" x 15½" piece *each* from one fabric, web, and poster board. Fuse fabric to poster board.
2. Fold one end of poster board piece 7" to wrong side.
3. For flap, fold remaining end of poster board piece 1¾" to wrong side. Cut one 1¾" x 5" piece *each* from remaining fabric and web. Fuse fabric piece to right side of flap. Staple bag of seasoning to wrong side of poster board under fold of flap.
4. Tie several lengths of raffia into a bow around barbeque tools; glue to top back of package.
5. Using supplies for gift tag, follow *Making a Tag*, page 122, to make gift tag. Glue tag to front of flap.

These savory butters are a delicious way to start the day off right! Seasoned with fresh basil, sage, or thyme, the creamy spreads are especially pleasing with oven-fresh rolls. For a charming country surprise, deliver your gift in a sponge-painted Shaker box — the checkerboard and cow accents are actually wallpaper motifs. How "udderly" delightful!

HERBED BUTTERS

   3 cups butter, softened and divided
   2 teaspoons finely chopped
       fresh basil, sage, *or* thyme
   1 cup whipping cream, divided

For *each* herbed butter, cream 1 cup butter in a medium bowl until fluffy using an electric mixer. With electric mixer running, add basil, sage, or thyme and gradually add $1/3$ cup whipping cream; beat until fluffy. Spoon into an airtight container. Cover and chill 4 hours to let flavors blend. Store in refrigerator.

Yield: about $1^{1}/_{2}$ cups of each herbed butter

COW BOX

You will need a 7" dia. Shaker box with lid; brown antiquing wash spray paint; ivory, green, brown, and black acrylic paint; sponge pieces; a section of prepasted wallpaper border with desired motif; matte Mod Podge® sealer; foam brush; and wood-tone spray.

1. Spray paint outside of box and lid with antiquing wash; allow to dry.
2. For box, using a dampened sponge piece and painting in the direction of the wood grain, paint box ivory. Follow *Sponge Painting*, page 123, and dip sponge piece in brown, then black paint to paint spots on box.
3. Dividing lid top along the wood grain, sponge paint top $1/2$ ivory, bottom $1/4$ brown, and remaining $1/4$ along center green; blend colors together while paint is still wet. Allow to dry.
4. Measure width of side of lid; measure around lid and add $1/2$". Cut a strip from wallpaper the determined measurements. Cut desired motif from wallpaper. Follow manufacturer's instructions to apply wallpaper strip to side of lid and motif to lid top.
5. Lightly spray box and lid with wood-tone spray.
6. Allowing to dry between coats, apply two to three coats of sealer to lid and box.

SAVORY BUTTERS

GARDEN-FRESH BREAD

VEGETABLE ROLL-UP BREAD WITH PESTO SPREAD

PESTO SPREAD
- 1 package (8 ounces) cream cheese, softened
- ½ cup coarsely chopped fresh basil leaves
- ¼ cup pine nuts, coarsely chopped
- 2 cloves garlic, minced
- ⅛ teaspoon salt

FILLING
- ⅓ cup shredded unpeeled zucchini
- ⅓ cup shredded carrots
- ⅓ cup finely chopped sweet red pepper
- 2 tablespoons finely chopped fresh parsley
- 2 tablespoons finely chopped green onions
- ¼ cup butter or margarine, softened
- ½ teaspoon salt
- ¼ teaspoon ground black pepper

BREAD
- 1 tablespoon sugar
- 1 package dry yeast
- 1½ cups warm water
- 3¼ to 3½ cups all-purpose flour, divided
- 1½ teaspoons salt
  Vegetable cooking spray
- 1 egg
- 1 tablespoon water

For pesto spread, process cream cheese, basil, pine nuts, garlic, and salt in a food processor until well blended. Store in an airtight container in refrigerator.

For filling, combine zucchini, carrots, red pepper, parsley, green onions, butter, salt, and black pepper in a medium bowl; stir until well blended. Cover and chill.

For bread, dissolve sugar and yeast in 1½ cups warm water in a small bowl. In a large bowl, combine 2 cups flour and salt. Add yeast mixture to dry ingredients; beat with an electric mixer until well blended. Add 1¼ cups flour, stir until a soft dough forms. Turn onto a lightly floured surface. Knead about 5 minutes or until dough becomes smooth and elastic, using additional flour as necessary. Place in a large bowl sprayed with cooking spray, turning once to coat top of dough. Cover and let rise in a warm place (80 to 85 degrees) about 1½ hours or until doubled in size.

Remove filling from refrigerator. Turn dough onto a lightly floured surface and punch down. Cover and let dough rest 10 minutes.

Divide dough in half. Roll one half into an 8 x 15-inch rectangle. Spread with half of filling. Beginning at 1 long edge, roll up dough jellyroll style. Pinch seam to seal. Pinch ends to seal and turn under dough. Repeat with remaining ingredients. Place each loaf on a lightly greased baking sheet. Spray tops with cooking spray. Cover and let rise in a warm place about 1 hour or until doubled in size.

Preheat oven to 350 degrees. In a small bowl, beat egg and 1 tablespoon water. Brush egg mixture over loaves. Bake 20 to 30 minutes or until golden brown. Serve warm or transfer to a wire rack to cool completely. Serve with pesto spread.

Yield: 2 loaves bread and 1¼ cups pesto spread

ROLL-UP BREAD GIFT BASKET

You will need a basket with vegetable motif and handle, fabric for liner, natural raffia, several sprigs of artificial greenery, and glue.

1. Follow *Making a Basket Liner*, page 124, to make liner with an unfinished edge.
2. Glue greenery sprigs to handle.
3. Covering ends of greenery sprigs, tie several lengths of raffia into a bow around handle.

During the summer's peak growing season, you'll have a bushel of opportunities to treat your friends to flavorful Vegetable Roll-up Bread. The tasty loaves are filled with fresh garden produce and served with creamy Pesto Spread. For convenience, present this wholesome offering in a ready-made basket.

NEIGHBORLY BREAKFAST BASKET

If you're "berry" pleased to meet your new neighbors, why not extend a hearty hello with a cheery breakfast basket! Loaded with a jar of luscious Strawberry-Mint Jam, freshly baked biscuits, simple fabric napkins, and easy-to-make napkin rings, this welcome-to-the-neighborhood surprise offers an eye-opening start to a day of unpacking.

STRAWBERRY-MINT JAM

    2 quarts fresh strawberries, coarsely
       chopped (about 6½ cups)
    ¼ cup coarsely chopped fresh mint
       leaves
    1 tablespoon freshly squeezed lemon
       juice
    1 package (1¾ ounces) powdered
       fruit pectin
    7 cups sugar

In a heavy Dutch oven, combine strawberries, mint leaves, lemon juice, and pectin over medium-high heat. Bring to a rolling boil. Add sugar. Stirring constantly, bring to a rolling boil again and boil 1 minute. Remove from heat; skim off foam. Spoon jam into heat-resistant jars; cover and cool to room temperature. Store in refrigerator.

Yield: about 7 cups jam

54

BREAKFAST BASKET

You will need a market basket (we used a 6½" x 14¼" basket), fabric for trim, two 22½" x 33" kitchen towels, four 2⅜" long silk strawberries, 1¼ yds of silk ivy garland, 1⅓ yds of ⅜"w ribbon, wire cutters, wood excelsior, and glue.
For jar lid, you will *also* need one 4" square each of fabric and batting.
For gift tag, you will *also* need red and yellow paper, black permanent felt-tip pen, decorative-edge craft scissors, and ivy leaves.

1. Measure around rim of basket; add 1". Measure width of rim. Tear a fabric strip the determined measurements. Glue fabric strip around rim. Place excelsior in basket.
2. For napkins, cut each towel in half widthwise. Fold raw edge of each towel half ¼" to wrong side. Fold ¼" to wrong side again and stitch in place.
3. For napkin rings, use wire cutters to cut ivy garland into four equal lengths; form each length into a circle. Twist ends together to secure.
4. Cut ribbon into four equal lengths. Tie each ribbon length into a bow around twisted ends of circle.
5. Glue one strawberry to each bow.
6. For jar lid, use fabric and batting squares and follow *Jar Lid Finishing*, page 122, to cover lid.
7. For gift tag, cut a 2" x 3⅜" piece of yellow paper. Glue yellow paper piece to red paper. Leaving a ¼" red border, use craft scissors to cut out gift tag. Use pen to write message on tag. Glue ivy leaves to tag.
8. Place gifts in basket.

FATHER'S DAY FUN

*D*ad will be quick
to show his appreciation for
this imaginative Father's Day
surprise! Rich, chewy Almond-
Amaretto Turtles are easy to
make, and you can decorate
the fun gift box while the
candies set. The clever carrier
features a poster board collar
and a wired-ribbon necktie.
Colored to match the ribbon,
a handmade tag completes
this handsome gift.

ALMOND-AMARETTO TURTLES

    3 cups whole almonds, toasted
    1 package (14 ounces) caramels
    1 teaspoon water
    5 teaspoons amaretto
    1 bar (7 ounces) mildly sweet dark
        chocolate, chopped
    6 ounces chocolate candy coating,
        chopped

On a greased baking sheet, place
4 almonds with ends touching to form a
cross. Repeat with remaining almonds.
Combine caramels and water in top of a
double boiler over simmering water; stir
until smooth. Stir in amaretto. Leave
caramel mixture over warm water; drop
1/2 teaspoonful over center of each
almond cluster. Melt chocolate and
candy coating in top of double boiler
over hot, not simmering, water. Remove
from heat. Spoon about 1 teaspoonful
chocolate over each caramel candy. Chill
candies 30 minutes or until chocolate
hardens. Store in an airtight container
in a cool place.

Yield: about 6 dozen candies

DAD'S DAY SHIRT BOX

You will need a white box (we used a
8¹/₂" x 11¹/₂" box), ³/₄ yd of 2¹/₂"w wired
ribbon, white poster board, two small
white buttons, tracing paper, and glue.
For gift tag, you will *also* need a
photocopy of tag design (page 119), blue
paper, brown and black markers, and
decorative-edge craft scissors.

1. Trace collar pattern, page 112, onto
tracing paper; cut out. Use pattern to cut
two shapes from poster board.

2. Tie one end of ribbon into a loose knot.
3. Glue knot to top of box. Trim long end
of ribbon to a point. Glue collar shapes at
each side of knot. Glue one button to each
collar point.
4. For gift tag, use brown marker to color
tag design. Use black marker to write
message on tag. Cut out tag.
5. Glue tag to blue paper. Leaving a ¹/₄"
blue border, use craft scissors to cut out
gift tag.

DO-DADDY SNACK MIX

On Father's Day, a gift of Do-Daddy Snack Mix offers a yummy reminder for Dad to do all the things he really enjoys — like putting his feet up and taking a nap! Baked with a buttery herb coating, the crunchy tidbits are perfect for Dad to nibble while watching TV. Our fabric-covered snack sack decorated with a fun "to do" list helps you button up this tasty surprise.

DO-DADDY SNACK MIX

$3/4$ cup butter or margarine
1 teaspoon dried oregano leaves
1 teaspoon dried marjoram leaves
1 teaspoon dried basil leaves
1 teaspoon dried parsley flakes
1 teaspoon dried minced onion
$1/2$ teaspoon garlic powder
$1/8$ teaspoon ground red pepper
1 package (14 ounces) oyster crackers
1 package (10 ounces) sesame and cheese snack sticks
1 package (10 ounces) cheese snack crackers
1 package ($8^1/2$ ounces) rippled cracker chips
1 package ($8^1/2$ ounces) wheat snack crackers

In a small microwave-safe bowl, combine butter, oregano, marjoram, basil, parsley, onion, garlic powder, and red pepper. Cover and microwave on medium-high power (80%) 1 minute. Stir and let mixture stand 10 minutes.

Preheat oven to 275 degrees. Divide the following evenly into 2 greased roasting pans: oyster crackers, sesame and cheese snack sticks, cheese snack crackers, rippled cracker chips, and wheat snack crackers. Pour half of butter mixture over each pan. Bake 30 minutes, stirring mixture and switching position of pans after 15 minutes. Spread on aluminum foil to cool. Store in an airtight container.

Yield: about 30 cups snack mix

FATHER'S DAY SNACK SACK

You will need a small brown paper grocery bag, fabric, paper-backed fusible web, 5" x $6^3/4$" torn cream colored handmade paper piece for label, 2" x $3^1/2$" torn cream colored handmade paper piece for tag, assorted buttons, black permanent felt-tip pen, black yarn, large-eye needle, hole punch, and glue.

1. Draw around front of bag on paper side of web. Fuse web to wrong side of fabric; cut out along drawn line. Fuse fabric piece to front of bag.
2. Use pen to write "Do-Daddy" message on label.
3. Punch two holes $2^1/2$" apart at center top of label. Thread a length of yarn through holes and knot at back of label. Glue label to front of bag. Glue buttons to label and front of bag.
4. Fold top of bag $1^1/2$" to front. Use pen to draw zigzag line and write message on tag. Sewing through corner of tag, use yarn and needle to sew button and tag to fold of bag. Knot ends of yarn at back of bag.

Help your friends welcome the fun summer season with this sunny picnic basket! Pack the carrier with hot dogs and all the fixings — including a jar of tangy Easy Hot Dog Relish. And since no picnic is complete without ants, why not use a marking pen to decorate the basket and liner with them!

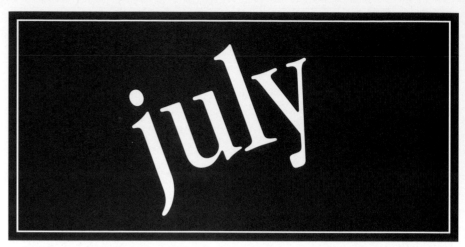

EASY HOT DOG RELISH

1 jar (16 ounces) dill pickle slices, drained
1 jar (9 ounces) prepared mustard
1/2 cup coarsely chopped onion
2 cloves garlic, coarsely chopped
2 teaspoons coarsely chopped fresh jalapeño pepper

Process pickles, mustard, onion, garlic, and jalapeño pepper in a food processor until pickles are coarsely chopped. Store in an airtight container in refrigerator.

Yield: about 2½ cups relish

PICNIC BASKET

You will need a square basket with handle (we used a 12" square basket), jar with a 4" dia. lid, fabric for basket liner, corded piping to coordinate with fabric, black paint pen, assorted silk flowers, paper napkin, tracing paper, transfer paper, 6" length of floral wire, and glue. *For jar lid label,* you will *also* need yellow and red paper, black permanent felt-tip pen, and serrated-edge craft scissors.

1. Measure around rim of basket; add 1". Cut a length of piping the determined measurement. Matching piping to bottom of rim, glue raw edge to basket.
2. For fabric liner, measure basket (Fig. 1); add 1". Cut a square of fabric the determined measurement.

Fig. 1

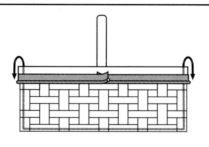

3. Trace ant pattern, page 113, onto tracing paper. Use transfer paper to transfer ants to basket handle and fabric liner. Use paint pen to paint ants; allow to dry.
4. Center fabric square in basket and press into corners. Trimming fabric to fit around handles and pleating fabric evenly at corners so that fabric lies flat in basket, fold edges of fabric over sides of basket.
5. Beginning at base of one handle, fold edges of fabric to wrong side so that folded edge of fabric covers raw edge of piping; glue in place.
6. Place flowers diagonally on napkin. Wrap wire length around flowers and napkin and twist ends at back of napkin. Twist wire ends around handle to secure to basket.
7. For jar lid label, trace pattern, page 113, on tracing paper. Use pattern to cut circle from yellow paper. Use transfer paper to transfer words to center of circle. Use felt-tip pen to draw over transferred words. Glue circle to red paper. Leaving a 1/4" red border, use craft scissors to cut out label. Glue label to jar lid.

HOT DOG PICNIC

TROPICAL FRUIT SHERBET

A *triple fruity frozen fantasy, Tropical Fruit Sherbet offers a fun salute to Air Conditioning Appreciation Day (July 3)! When the dog days of summer arrive, this chilly confection gives you a cool reason to get together with the gang and enjoy the beauty of the great indoors! Add fun to the festivities by presenting the freezer pleaser in a colorful no-sew basket along with whimsical ice cream dishes.*

TROPICAL FRUIT SHERBET

    1 fresh pineapple, peeled and
         cored
    3 passion fruit
    4 kiwi fruit, peeled and sliced
    1 envelope unflavored gelatin
  1/4 cup cold water
    1 cup whole milk, divided
  3/4 cup sugar, divided
    1 can (8 1/2 ounces) cream of
         coconut
    2 tablespoons freshly squeezed
         lemon juice

Process pineapple in food processor until puréed. Transfer to a medium saucepan. Stirring occasionally, cook over medium heat 8 minutes; remove from heat.

In a small bowl, scrape seeds and yellow pulp from skin of passion fruit; discard skin. Purée passion fruit and kiwi fruit in a food processor; strain to remove seeds. In a heavy large saucepan, sprinkle gelatin over water; soften 1 minute. Stir in 1/2 cup milk and 1/4 cup sugar. Stirring constantly, cook over low heat until gelatin dissolves. Stir in remaining 1/2 cup milk and remaining 1/2 cup sugar. Stirring frequently, cook over medium-low heat until sugar dissolves. Remove from heat; stir in fruit, cream of coconut, and lemon juice. Transfer to a metal or plastic bowl. Cover and freeze overnight.

Let mixture stand at room temperature 1 hour. Break into pieces and process in a large food processor until smooth; refreeze in an airtight container. Serve frozen.

Yield: about 7 1/2 cups sherbet

FABRIC-COVERED BASKET

You will need a round basket with handle (we used an 11" dia. basket), fabric to cover basket, two rubber bands, natural excelsior, and glue.

For gift tag, you will *also* need a photocopy of tag design (page 119), green paper, 1/3 yd of 1/8"w pink ribbon, purple and green colored pencils, decorative-edge craft scissors, black permanent felt-tip pen, and a hole punch.

1. Center basket on wrong side of fabric.
2. Pulling fabric taut, gather fabric at base of handle on each side of basket; use rubber bands to secure gathers. Tuck ends of fabric and rubber bands between basket and fabric; glue at handle to secure. Turn remaining fabric edges to wrong side with fold even with top of basket; glue to secure.
3. For gift tag, use pencils to color tag design. Cut out tag. Use pen to write message on tag. Glue tag to green paper. Leaving a 3/8" green border, use craft scissors to cut out gift tag.
4. Use hole punch to punch hole in tag. Loop ribbon through hole and tie ribbon into a bow around basket handle.

MADE-IN-THE-SHADE LEMONADE

*O*n *Stay Out of the Sun Day (July 3), why not throw an indoor beach party for your friends and give their skin a break from the intense summer rays! To get the gathering off to a great start, give each guest a fun-to-wear sun visor, then serve lots of zippy Fresh Mint Lemonade. Keep the party spirit going by adding a sunny label to the beverage container.*

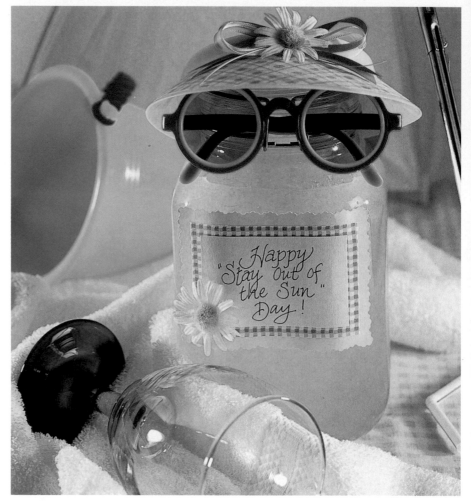

FRESH MINT LEMONADE

- 6 cups sugar
- 2 cups water
- 2 cups coarsely chopped fresh mint leaves
- 3 cups freshly squeezed lemon juice (about 16 lemons)
- 2 tablespoons grated lemon zest

In a Dutch oven, combine sugar and water over medium heat; stir until sugar dissolves. Increase heat to medium-high. Add mint leaves and bring to a boil. Stirring constantly, boil 1 minute. Strain syrup into a heat-resistant container; allow to cool. Stir in lemon juice and lemon zest. Cover and chill. Give with serving instructions.

Yield: about 8 cups lemonade concentrate

To serve: Combine 2 parts club soda with 1 part lemonade concentrate. Serve over ice; garnish with lemon slices and mint leaves.

SUMMERTIME JAR

You will need a ¹/₂-gallon glass jar with wire-hinged lid, plastic visor, fabric, ¹/₃ yd each of two ¹/₄"w and one ¹/₈"w ribbons, two artificial daisies, sunglasses, tracing paper, and glue.

For jar label you will *also* need a 2" x 3¹/₄" white paper piece, yellow paper, decorative-edge craft scissors, and a black permanent felt-tip pen.

1. For visor, trace brim of visor onto tracing paper; cut out.
2. Trace around pattern on wrong side of fabric. Cutting ¹/₄" inside drawn line, cut out shape. Glue shape to visor.
3. Tie ribbon lengths into a bow and glue to visor. Glue daisy to knot of bow .
4. For jar label, glue white paper piece to fabric. Leaving a ¹/₄" fabric border, cut around white paper piece. Glue fabric to yellow paper. Leaving a ¹/₄" yellow border, use craft scissors to cut out label.
5. Use pen to write message on label. Glue label to jar. Glue daisy to label.
6. Place temples of sunglasses through hinge of jar lid. Place visor on jar.

CHILLED GARDEN SOUP

*T*here's a gardenful
of goodness in every bite of
our delicious Chilled Garden
Soup! Made with a variety of
fresh vegetables, it's a luscious
low-fat dish that's ideal for
a light summertime supper.
A batch of soup and a pair of
veggie-motif mugs make a nice
seasonal surprise for a friend
who enjoys wholesome,
just-picked produce. As a
thoughtful touch, line your
gift basket with a cotton
kitchen towel and tie on
a vegetable-print bow
embellished with a silk
flower and faux greenery.

CHILLED GARDEN SOUP

     1   medium eggplant, peeled
             and cut into $1/2$-inch cubes
             (about 5 cups)
     2   medium yellow squash halved
             lengthwise and thinly sliced
             (about 3 cups)
$11/3$ cups finely chopped green pepper
     1   cup fresh or frozen whole kernel
             corn
     1   cup fresh or frozen green peas
     1   cup thinly sliced carrots
  $1/2$ cup finely chopped celery
  $1/3$ cup finely chopped green onions
  $1/4$ cup chopped fresh parsley
     2   tablespoons olive oil
     1   clove garlic, minced
     2   cans ($141/2$ ounces each) fat-free
             chicken broth
     3   cups peeled and coarsely chopped
             fresh plum tomatoes
     2   tablespoons red wine vinegar

     1   teaspoon salt
  $1/2$ teaspoon ground white pepper
  $1/4$ teaspoon hot pepper sauce

In a Dutch oven over medium heat,
combine eggplant, squash, green pepper,
corn, peas, carrots, celery, green onions,
parsley, oil, and garlic. Cover and cook
about 15 minutes or until eggplant is
tender, stirring frequently. Add chicken
broth, tomatoes, vinegar, salt, white
pepper, and pepper sauce; bring to a boil.
Reduce heat to medium-low; cover and
cook about 15 to 20 minutes. Store in
refrigerator in an airtight container. Serve
chilled.
Yield: about 12 cups soup

ALL-AMERICAN MUFFINS

This Fourth of July, salute great all-American tastes with our spectacular Red-White-and-Blue Muffins! Maraschino cherries, vanilla baking chips, and fresh blueberries are baked into the moist little cakes for bite after bite of star-spangled flavor. For a dandy delivery, use a flag-inspired painted plate to take the muffins to a get-together.

RED-WHITE-AND-BLUE MUFFINS

    2   cups all-purpose flour
    1   cup quick-cooking oats
  1/3   cup firmly packed brown sugar
  1/3   cup granulated sugar
  3/4   teaspoon baking soda
  3/4   teaspoon baking powder
  1/4   teaspoon salt
  3/4   cup buttermilk
  1/2   cup butter or margarine, melted
    2   eggs
    1   teaspoon vanilla extract
    1   package (12 ounces) vanilla
          baking chips
    1   cup coarsely chopped maraschino
          cherries
    1   cup fresh blueberries

Preheat oven to 375 degrees. In a large bowl, combine flour, oats, sugars, baking soda, baking powder, and salt. Form a well in center of dry ingredients. In a small bowl, combine buttermilk, melted butter, eggs, and vanilla. Add liquid to dry ingredients; stir just until moistened. Stir in vanilla chips, cherries, and blueberries.

Fill paper-lined muffin cups two-thirds full. Bake 18 to 22 minutes or until lightly browned. Transfer muffins to a wire rack to cool. Store in an airtight container.

Yield: about 2 dozen muffins

FLAG PLATE

Caution: Plate is for decorative use only and is not intended for direct contact with food.

You will need a 10" dia. unfinished wooden plate; white, red, and blue acrylic paint; satin clear acrylic spray sealer; foam brush; paintbrushes; tracing paper; transfer paper; facial tissues; and sandpaper.

Refer to Painting Techniques, page 123, for painting tips.

1. Sand plate, wash with soap and water, and allow to dry.
2. Use foam brush to paint plate white; allow to dry.
3. Trace stars and swirls pattern, page 112, onto tracing paper. Aligning curve of pattern with edge of plate, use transfer paper to transfer background outline (shown in blue) to plate. Use a pencil to draw stripes on plate as desired.
4. Paint background area blue and stripes red. Before paint dries, lightly blot paint with tissues using a clean area of tissue each time.
5. Transfer stars and swirls to blue section of plate. Paint stars and swirls white.
6. Allowing to dry between coats, apply two to three coats of sealer to plate.
7. Wipe plate with a damp cloth after each use.

REVOLUTIONARY SALSA

*D*eclare your independence from ordinary chips and dip! Our Tangy Peach Salsa promises to set off a sweet-and-spicy taste revolution that will please Democrats and Republicans alike. Pack the sassy salsa in a star-spangled gift basket along with crispy tortilla chips for sharing.

TANGY PEACH SALSA

- 3 cups peeled and finely chopped fresh peaches (about 5 peaches)
- 2 tablespoons honey
- 1 tablespoon minced onion
- 1 tablespoon freshly squeezed lime juice
- 1 tablespoon chopped fresh cilantro
- 1 tablespoon sugar
- 1 small jalapeño pepper, seeded and finely chopped
- 2 teaspoons chopped crystallized ginger
- 1/8 teaspoon salt
  Tortilla chips to serve

In a medium nonmetal bowl, combine peaches, honey, onion, lime juice, cilantro, sugar, jalapeño pepper, ginger, and salt. Store in an airtight container in refrigerator. Serve with tortilla chips or as a condiment with meat.

Yield: about 3 cups salsa

FESTIVE FOURTH OF JULY BASKET

You will need a red market basket with handle, white tissue paper, star garland, 20" length of 1¹/₂"w red and white check grosgrain ribbon, and flag-motif paper napkins.

For chip bag, you will *also* need a small white paper bag; red and white stripe fabric; paper-backed fusible web; hole punch; and red, white, and blue curling ribbon.

1. For chip bag, draw around front of bag on paper side of web. Fuse web to wrong side of fabric. Cut out along drawn lines.

Fuse fabric piece to front of bag. Place tortilla chips in bag.

2. Fold top of bag 1¹/₂" to front. Punch two holes 1" apart at center top of bag. Thread several lengths of curling ribbon through holes and tie into a bow at front of bag; curl ends.

3. Line basket with tissue paper. Place bag, napkins, and salsa in basket. Arrange garland around basket. Twist ends around handle to secure. Tie ribbon into a bow around handle.

*H*ere's an appetizing gift that's sure to catch the attention of a fish lover! Served with toast or crackers, Tasty Catfish Spread makes a wonderful snack, especially during National Catfish Month (August). And there's nothing fishy about how easy it is to put together the clever bag — just draw the details on a paper sack. Next, add a few ribbon whiskers and a twisted paper tail and fins for "reel" appeal.

TASTY CATFISH SPREAD

    2   pounds catfish fillets
        Salt and ground white pepper
    1   cup sour cream
  1/2   cup mayonnaise
  1/2   cup finely chopped celery
  1/2   cup finely chopped green onions
  1/4   cup finely chopped fresh parsley
    1   jar (2 ounces) diced pimiento,
          drained
    3   tablespoons freshly squeezed
          lemon juice
    1   tablespoon chopped fresh dill weed
    1   tablespoon prepared horseradish
  1/2   teaspoon salt
        Toast points or crackers to serve

Preheat oven to 350 degrees. Place fish on a lightly greased 10½ x 15½-inch jellyroll pan. Lightly sprinkle salt and white pepper over fish. Bake about 20 minutes or until fish flakes easily when tested with a fork. Remove from oven and cool. Transfer fish to an airtight container and chill 1 hour or until thoroughly chilled.

In a medium bowl, combine sour cream, mayonnaise, celery, green onions, parsley, pimiento, lemon juice, dill weed, horseradish, and ½ teaspoon salt; stir until well blended. Break chilled fish into pieces. Gently fold fish into mayonnaise mixture. Cover and chill 4 hours to let flavors blend. Serve chilled with toast points or crackers.

Yield: about 5 cups spread

CATFISH BAG

You will need a brown paper bottle bag, 10" length of ⅛"w black ribbon, black paper twist (untwisted), black permanent felt-tip pen, black colored pencil, 4" length of floral wire, hole punch, and glue.

1. For snout, leaving 1" of center bottom of bag unfolded, fold corners diagonally to back. Glue folds to secure.
2. Use pen to draw eye, gill, mouth, and body details on bag as desired. Shade bag with colored pencil.
3. Punch hole 1" from end of snout. Leaving a 1" tail extending beyond knot, knot ribbon ends together. Thread ends from front to back through hole in bag. Glue ends to back of bag to secure. Cut loop in ribbon.
4. Cut fin and tail shapes from untwisted paper. Glue fins to bag.
5. Place gift in bag.
6. Tightly gather open end of bag; use wire to secure. Glue tail shape to bag, covering wire.

TASTY CATFISH SPREAD

MIDSUMMER DELIGHT

*F*or a unique reminder
of the season's goodness, give
jars of Watermelon Rind
Preserves on August 7 — the
official midpoint of summer.
The sweet, spicy condiment is
great for warm-weather picnics
or for snacking any time of the
year. A little flowerpot that's
sponge-painted to resemble
the season's most popular
fruit adds fun to your gift.

WATERMELON RIND PRESERVES

1 watermelon (about 18 to
    20 pounds) to yield about
    4 pounds of rind
3 quarts water
6 tablespoons canning and pickling
    salt
2 quarts water
8 cups sugar
2 lemons, thinly sliced
2 teaspoons ground cinnamon
1 teaspoon ground ginger

Cut watermelon into 8 pieces. Remove
all but 1/4 inch of pink flesh; peel
watermelon. Cut rind into 1-inch cubes.
In a large nonmetal bowl, combine
3 quarts water and salt. Place rind in salt
water. Cover and let stand 5 hours.

Using a colander, drain and thoroughly
rinse rind with cold water. Return rind to
large bowl and cover with cold water; let
stand 30 minutes.

Drain again and place rind in a large
enamelware Dutch oven; cover with cold
water. Bring to a boil over high heat.
Reduce heat to medium and simmer
30 minutes or until tender; drain in
colander. In Dutch oven, combine
2 quarts water and sugar. Over high heat,
bring sugar mixture to a boil; boil
5 minutes. Reduce heat to medium. Add
rind to sugar syrup; continue to gently
boil 30 minutes. Add lemon slices,
cinnamon, and ginger; continue cooking
about 2 hours longer or until rind is
almost translucent. Spoon preserves into
heat-resistant jars; cover and cool to
room temperature. Store in refrigerator.

Yield: about 4 pints preserves

WATERMELON POT AND JAR LID

You will need a 5"h clay flowerpot;
red, yellow-green, dark green, and
black acrylic paint; paintbrushes;
compressed craft sponge; spray primer;
clear acrylic spray sealer; tracing paper;
raffia; green excelsior; and a 7 1/2" dia.
pinked fabric circle.
For gift tag, you will *also* need a
photocopy of tag design (page 119), red
paper, colored markers, decorative-edge
craft scissors, and glue.

*Refer to Painting Techniques, page 123,
for painting tips. Allow to dry after each
paint application.*

1. Trace watermelon pattern, page 113,
onto tracing paper; cut out. Use pattern
to cut shape from sponge.
2. Spray pot with primer.
3. Paint outside of pot yellow-green.
4. Follow *Sponge Painting,* page 123, to
paint red watermelons on rim and dark
green stripes on pot below rim.
5. Paint black seeds on watermelons.
6. Apply two to three coats of sealer
to pot.
7. Line pot with excelsior.
8. Place fabric circle over jar lid. Knot
several lengths of raffia around jar lid and
fabric circle.
9. For gift tag, use markers to color tag
design and to write message on tag. Cut
out tag.
10. Glue tag to red paper. Leaving an
1/8" red border, use craft scissors to cut
out gift tag.

FRIENDSHIP HERB CANDIES

*I*t's been said that friends are the flowers that bloom in life's garden. So why not offer gifts of citrusy Herb Candies to your special pals as sweet reminders of how important they are to you! Tied with shimmering iridescent ribbon, pretty glass jars are great for showing off the treats. Hand-crafted gift tags and sprays of flowers will help your friendships grow.

HERB CANDIES

We made two recipes, one with each herb.

1²/₃ cups sugar
²/₃ cup light corn syrup
¹/₂ cup water
3 tablespoons chopped fresh tarragon leaves *or* thyme leaves
2 teaspoons orange extract *or* lemon extract
Red and yellow liquid food coloring (for tarragon candy only)

For tarragon candy, combine sugar, corn syrup, and water in a heavy medium saucepan. Stirring constantly, cook over medium-low heat until sugar dissolves. Using a pastry brush dipped in hot water, wash down any sugar crystals on sides of pan. Attach a candy thermometer to pan, making sure thermometer does not touch bottom of pan. Increase heat to medium-high and bring to a boil. Cook, without stirring, until mixture reaches

280 degrees. Test about ¹/₂ teaspoon mixture in ice water. Mixture will form hard threads in ice water but will soften when removed from the water. Remove from heat. Add tarragon, orange extract, and 4 drops red and 2 drops yellow food coloring. Drop ¹/₂ teaspoonfuls of candy

onto greased aluminum foil (if candy in pan begins to harden, return to heat). Allow candy to cool completely. Store in an airtight container.

For thyme candy, repeat the above directions using thyme and lemon extract.

Yield: about 10 dozen pieces candy

70

CHOCOLATE FUDGE PIE

*A*ny day is the right day to share our decadent Chocolate Fudge Pie with a chocolate lover! The satiny treat is packed with chocolate chips and rich pecan bits. Edible chocolate hearts add a fun finish to this fabulous dessert. For a cute delivery, a torn-fabric liner is decorated with ribbon and felt hearts, and a simple card announces your gift.

CHOCOLATE FUDGE PIE

- 1 unbaked 9-inch pie crust
- $^1/_2$ cup butter or margarine
- 1 package (6 ounces) chocolate chips, divided
- 1 cup sugar
- 3 tablespoons all-purpose flour
- 3 eggs
- 1 cup finely chopped pecans
- 1 teaspoon vanilla extract

Preheat oven to 400 degrees. Bake pie crust 5 minutes. Remove from oven; reduce temperature to 325 degrees.

In a heavy medium saucepan, melt butter and $^3/_4$ cup chocolate chips over low heat. In a medium bowl, combine chocolate mixture, sugar, and flour; beat until well blended. Add eggs, 1 at a time, beating well after each addition. Stir in pecans and vanilla. Pour filling into pie crust. Bake 40 to 50 minutes or until filling is firm. Transfer to a wire rack to cool.

Line a baking sheet with aluminum foil; grease foil. In a heavy small saucepan, melt remaining $^1/_4$ cup chocolate chips over low heat. Pour melted chocolate onto prepared baking sheet. Chill 30 minutes or until chocolate hardens. Use a $1^1/_8$-inch-wide heart-shaped cookie cutter to cut out chocolate hearts. Chill hearts about 5 minutes or until firm. Place chocolate hearts on warm pie; cool. Store in an airtight container in refrigerator.

Yield: about 8 servings

CHOCOLATE LOVER GIFT TAG

You will need cream colored handmade paper, brown paper, brown permanent felt-tip pen, 8" length of $^1/_4$"w grosgrain ribbon, and glue.

1. Tear a 2" x $3^1/_2$" piece from handmade paper. Use pen to write message on paper piece. Glue paper piece to brown paper. Cutting close to handmade paper piece, cut out gift tag.
2. Tie ribbon into a bow; glue to corner of tag.

COOL SUMMER DIP

*O*ne of the joys of summer is sharing the bounty of your garden. Made with fresh veggies, cool Radish Dip is especially flavorful served with easy-to-make Rye Chips. For an imaginative presentation, line a market basket with a stenciled cloth and tuck in a jar of dip and a bag of chips.

RADISH DIP WITH RYE CHIPS

  1 container (8 ounces) sour cream
  1 cup shredded or finely chopped
      radishes
$1/2$ cup mayonnaise
$1/3$ cup finely chopped celery
  2 teaspoons dried chives
  2 teaspoons cream-style horseradish
$1/4$ teaspoon salt
  1 loaf (16 ounces) sliced cocktail
      rye bread
$3^{1}/_{2}$ tablespoons olive oil

In a medium bowl, combine sour cream, radishes, mayonnaise, celery, chives, horseradish, and salt. Cover and chill 2 hours to let flavors blend.

Preheat oven to 300 degrees. Brush bread slices with oil. Cut each slice in half diagonally to form 2 triangles. Place bread triangles on a baking sheet. Bake 25 minutes or until bread is crisp, turning pieces after 15 minutes. Cool rye chips on baking sheet. Store in an airtight container.

Yield: about 2 cups dip and about $7^{1}/_{2}$ dozen chips

RADISH BASKET

You will need a basket (we used a $5^{1}/_{2}$" x $9^{1}/_{2}$" basket), torn muslin piece large enough to line and drape over sides of basket, torn fabric piece slightly larger than muslin piece, red and green acrylic paint, stencil plastic, craft knife and cutting mat, stencil brushes, and black permanent felt-tip pen.

1. Use radish pattern, page 113, and follow *Stenciling,* page 123, to stencil red radishes and green leaves at each corner of muslin piece.
2. Use pen to outline and draw detail lines on radishes and leaves, and to draw "stitches" along edges of muslin piece.
3. Center muslin piece on remaining fabric piece and place in basket.

FRIENDSHIP HARVEST

*D*uring the summer months, patient gardeners are rewarded with bushels of fresh produce — especially fast-ripening tomatoes. For a decidedly different way to share your abundant harvest, why not prepare several batches of tasty Tomato-Basil Jam to give to friends. "Planted" in a beribboned basket, a jar of jam and some home-baked biscuits are just the things to help your friendship grow!

TOMATO-BASIL JAM

The cooking time of tomatoes may vary due to amount of juice.

- 3 pounds plum tomatoes, peeled and chopped (about 7 cups)
- 1/2 cup chopped fresh basil leaves
- 3 tablespoons freshly squeezed lemon juice
- 1 package (1³/₄ ounces) powdered fruit pectin
- 5 cups sugar

In a heavy Dutch oven, bring tomatoes to a boil over medium-high heat. Reduce heat to medium-low. Simmer about 30 minutes or until tomatoes reduce to 4 cups of tomatoes and juice. Increase heat to medium-high and stir in basil, lemon juice, and pectin. Bring to a rolling boil. Add sugar. Stirring constantly, bring to a rolling boil again and boil 1 minute. Remove from heat; skim off foam. Spoon jam into heat-resistant jars; cover and cool to room temperature. Store in refrigerator.

Yield: about 7 cups jam

TWIG BASKET AND JAR LABEL

You will need a twig basket, fabric to line basket, 2¹/₄"w wired ribbon, raffia, floral wire, wire cutters, 6" length of silk ivy garland, decorative shovel, and glue. *For jar label*, you will *also* need a photocopy of tag design (page 119), and red permanent felt-tip pen.

1. Measure around basket; add ¹/₂". Cut a length of ribbon the determined measurement. Glue ribbon length around basket. Line basket with fabric.

2. For ornament, tie a 36" length of ribbon into a bow. Tie several lengths of raffia into a bow. Aligning centers, stack ribbon bow, ivy, and then raffia bow together. Wrap wire around centers of bows and ivy. Twist wire ends at back of ribbon bow to secure. Glue bow to shovel handle.

3. For jar label, cut out tag design. Use pen to write "Tomato-Basil Jam" on tag. Glue tag to jar.

Brown bagging it back to school doesn't have to be boring! Liven up your child's lunchtime with tasty morsels such as creamy Veggie Dip with vegetable sticks, Bologna and Cheese Sandwich Spread, and crispy Chocolate Slice and Bake Cookies — all packed in a cool canvas lunch bag. The sturdy carrier is as easy as A-B-C to decorate using fusible letters, rubber stamps, buttons, and other simple craft supplies.

VEGGIE DIP

  1 package (8 ounces) cream cheese, softened
  1/4 cup Thousand Island salad dressing
    Carrot and celery sticks to serve

In a small bowl, beat cream cheese until fluffy. Add salad dressing and beat until well blended. Cover and chill 4 hours to let flavors blend. Serve with carrot and celery sticks.

Yield: about 1 1/4 cups dip

BOLOGNA AND CHEESE SANDWICH SPREAD

  1 1/2 pounds bologna, cut into pieces
  8 ounces American cheese, cut into pieces
  1 cup mayonnaise
  3/4 cup sweet pickle relish
  1/4 teaspoon salt
  1/4 teaspoon ground black pepper

Pulse process bologna, cheese, mayonnaise, pickle relish, salt, and pepper in a large food processor just until

blended. Cover and store in an airtight container in refrigerator.

Yield: about 5 cups sandwich spread

CHOCOLATE SLICE AND BAKE COOKIES

Cookie dough may be made ahead and frozen.

  3/4 cup butter or margarine, softened
  1 cup sugar
  1 egg
  1 teaspoon vanilla extract
  2 cups all-purpose flour
  1/4 cup cocoa
  1/2 teaspoon baking soda
  1/4 teaspoon salt

In a medium bowl, cream butter and sugar until fluffy. Add egg and vanilla; beat until well blended. In a small bowl, combine flour, cocoa, baking soda, and salt. Add dry ingredients to creamed mixture; stir until a soft dough forms. Cover and chill 30 minutes.

Divide dough in half. Shape each half into an 8-inch-long roll. Wrap in plastic wrap and chill 1 hour.

Preheat oven to 350 degrees. Cut dough into 1/4-inch slices and place 1 inch apart on an ungreased baking sheet. Bake 7 to 9 minutes or until

bottoms are lightly browned. Transfer cookies to a wire rack to cool. Store in an airtight container.

Yield: about 5 dozen cookies

SCHOOL LUNCH BAG

You will need a canvas lunch bag with handles and zippered opening (we used a 9" x 6" x 6"h bag), 3/4"h fusible letters, assorted school-theme rubber stamps, stamp pad, acrylic paint, paintbrushes, black permanent felt-tip pen, assorted buttons, embroidery floss to contrast with buttons, 7/8 yd of 1"w ribbon, 1"w paper-backed fusible web tape, glue, ABC wooden cutout, and a 5"l ball chain.

1. Follow manufacturer's instructions to fuse letters to front of lunch bag to spell out "LUNCH TIME."
2. Use rubber stamps and stamp pad to stamp designs on lunch bag. Paint designs as desired; allow to dry. Use pen to outline and draw details on designs.
3. Thread floss through button holes and knot at back. Glue buttons on lunch bag.
4. Follow manufacturer's instructions to fuse web tape to ribbon. Cut ribbon length in half. Fuse ribbon to handles on bag.
5. Paint wooden cutout; allow to dry. Use ball chain to attach cutout to zipper pull of lunch bag.

SUMMER RELISH

*A*s Labor Day approaches, we all relish the thought of one last summer party. Why not spice up your get-together by serving tangy Green Tomato Relish! The spicy condiment is delicious with a variety of meats and vegetables. To surprise your guests, favor them with take-home jars of relish topped with cross-stitched lids. A purchased basket and colorful ribbon complete your gifts.

GREEN TOMATO RELISH

     4   pounds firm green tomatoes, finely chopped (about 8 cups)
     1   pound onions, finely chopped
     1   green pepper, finely chopped
     1   sweet red pepper, finely chopped
    ½   small jalapeño pepper, seeded and finely chopped
    ⅓   cup canning and pickling salt
    1⅓   cups white vinegar
    1⅓   cups apple cider vinegar
     1   cup sugar
     1   tablespoon pickling spice tied in cheesecloth

In a large non-aluminum bowl, combine tomatoes, onions, and peppers. Stir in pickling salt. Cover and let stand at room temperature overnight.

Pour vegetables into a colander; rinse and press liquid out of vegetables. In a large non-aluminum stockpot, combine vinegars, sugar, and pickling spice over medium-high heat. Bring to a boil. Add vegetables and reduce heat to medium-low; simmer about 30 minutes or until

vegetables are tender. Remove spice bag and discard. Spoon relish into heat-resistant jars; cover and cool to room temperature. Store in refrigerator.

Yield: about 9 cups relish

CROSS-STITCH JAR LID

You will need a 6" square of White Aida (14 ct); embroidery floss (see color key, page 113); and ⅓ yd each of one ⅜"w, two ⅛"w, and one 1/16"w ribbons.

1. Using three strands of floss for Cross Stitch and two strands of floss for Backstitch and French Knot, follow *Cross Stitch* and *Embroidery*, page 124, to center and stitch jar lid design, page 113, on Aida.

2. For jar lid insert, use flat part of a jar lid (same size as jar lid used in storing food) as a pattern to cut design from Aida. Follow Step 2 of *Jar Lid Finishing*, page 122, to place lid on jar.

3. Knot ribbon lengths around lid.

SPORTSMAN'S SNACK PACK

A favorite sportsman can kick off National Hunting and Fishing Day (the fourth Saturday in September) with this savory snack pack. A wilderness staple, the smoky Meat Jerky can be made with beef or venison. For delivery, stow the jerky in a camouflage bag and then pack it in a rustic basket trimmed with hunting supplies.

MEAT JERKY

1³/₄ pounds flank steak
3 tablespoons soy sauce
3 tablespoons Worcestershire sauce
1 teaspoon liquid smoke
¹/₂ teaspoon garlic salt
¹/₂ teaspoon onion powder
¹/₄ teaspoon ground black pepper

For easier slicing, freeze steak 30 minutes. In a small bowl, combine soy sauce, Worcestershire sauce, liquid smoke, garlic salt, onion powder, and pepper. Slice steak across the grain into ¹/₄-inch slices. Place steak in a resealable plastic bag. Pour marinade over steak. Store in refrigerator overnight, turning occasionally to marinate meat.

Preheat oven to 140 degrees. Place meat strips on a wire rack over a jellyroll pan. Bake 10 to 12 hours or until a piece of cooled meat cracks when bent. Allow meat to cool. Store in an airtight container in refrigerator.

Yield: about 14 ounces meat jerky

CAMOUFLAGE BAG AND BASKET

You will need an 11¹/₂" x 30" piece of camouflage fabric, twig basket (we used a 6" x 9" basket), three spent shotgun shells, two large buttons, 1 yd jute twine, and glue.

For gift tag, you will *also* a need photocopy of tag design (page 119), green paper, black felt-tip pen, brown colored pencil, and decorative-edge craft scissors.

1. Follow *Making a Sewn Fabric Bag,* page 123, to make bag from fabric piece.
2. Center and sew one button 1¹/₂" from top on one side of bag (back). Sew remaining button 5" from bottom on front of bag.
3. For bag closure, wrap one end of twine several times around one shell; glue to secure. Repeat for opposite end of twine.
4. Place gift in bag. Fold top of bag 4" to front. Loop twine several times around buttons to secure. Tuck side edges of flap to inside.
5. Place bag in basket. Glue remaining shell to basket.
6. Using supplies for gift tag, follow *Making a Tag,* page 122, to make gift tag.

AUTUMN CARROT-ORANGE CONSERVE

*T*he first day of fall is a wonderful occasion to share gifts of Spicy Carrot-Orange Conserve. Prepared with fresh carrots, orange juice, and walnuts, the tangy mixture is delicious with a variety of meats. For a dazzling presentation, embellish a ready-made bag with silk leaves, gold-trimmed ribbon, and a hand-lettered gift tag.

SPICY CARROT-ORANGE CONSERVE

- 2 pounds carrots, peeled and shredded
- 3 cups water
- 2$^1/_2$ cups sugar
- 1 cup golden raisins
- $^2/_3$ cup orange juice
- 2 tablespoons finely chopped crystallized ginger
- 1 tablespoon grated orange zest
- 1$^1/_2$ teaspoons ground cinnamon
- 1 cup finely chopped walnuts

In a Dutch oven, combine carrots, water, sugar, raisins, and orange juice. Bring mixture to a boil over medium-high heat. Reduce heat to medium-low. Stir in ginger, orange zest, and cinnamon; simmer uncovered about 50 minutes or until carrots and raisins are tender and mixture thickens. Stir in walnuts. Spoon conserve into heat-resistant jars; cover and cool to room temperature. Store in refrigerator. Serve with meat or poultry.

Yield: about 7$^1/_2$ cups conserve

To go with your favorite meat
SPICY CARROT-ORANGE CONSERVE

APPRECIATION PIE

Really good neighbors are more than just the folks who live next door — they're good friends, too. Take time to say "thank you" to these great people with a gift of Graham Toffee Pie, a fluffy dessert loaded with rich pecans. A handmade tag makes this thoughtful surprise even more special.

GRAHAM TOFFEE PIE

8 graham crackers (2¹/₂ x 5 inches each)

¹/₃ cup firmly packed brown sugar

¹/₃ cup butter

4 egg whites

1 cup plus 2 tablespoons granulated sugar, divided

1 teaspoon vanilla extract

¹/₂ teaspoon cream of tartar

¹/₈ teaspoon salt

1 cup chopped pecans, toasted

1 cup whipping cream

Preheat oven to 350 degrees. Place crackers in a single layer on a 10¹/₂ x 15¹/₂-inch jellyroll pan. In a heavy small saucepan, combine brown sugar and butter. Stirring constantly, cook over medium heat until sugar dissolves and mixture begins to boil. Without stirring, boil 3 minutes. Pour syrup evenly over crackers, spreading to cover crackers. Bake 5 to 7 minutes or until syrup is bubbly and crackers are slightly browned around edges. Cool completely in pan. Break crackers into small pieces.

Reduce oven to 325 degrees. In a medium bowl, beat egg whites until foamy. Gradually add 1 cup granulated sugar,

vanilla, cream of tartar, and salt; continue beating until stiff peaks form. Fold in cracker pieces and pecans. Spoon mixture into a greased and lightly floured 9-inch pie plate. Bake 40 to 50 minutes or until filling is set and top is lightly browned. Cool on a wire rack.

Beat whipping cream until frothy. Gradually add remaining 2 tablespoons granulated sugar; beat until stiff peaks form. Spread whipped cream over top of pie. Store in an airtight container in refrigerator.

Yield: 8 to 10 servings

GREAT NEIGHBOR GIFT BOX AND TAG

You will need a 10" x 10" x 4" pie box, wrapping paper, spray adhesive, and 2 yds of 2¹/₄"w wired paper ribbon.

For gift tag, you will *also* need a photocopy of tag design (page 113), 3⁵/₈" x 5³/₈" piece of cardboard, colored pencils, black permanent felt-tip pen, ruler, hole punch, 6" length of jute twine, and glue.

1. Follow *Covering a Box*, page 124, to cover pie box.
2. Place pie in box. Tie ribbon into a bow around box.
3. For gift tag, use colored pencils to color tag design. Cut out tag.
4. Center and glue tag to cardboard. Use pen and ruler to draw lines around tag. Draw a heart at each corner of drawn lines.
5. Punch hole in corner of tag. Loop twine through hole. Tie gift tag to ribbon on box.

NUTTY CHICKEN-BROCCOLI SALAD

I f you have a good friend who's nuts about chicken, our Nutty Chicken-Broccoli Salad will certainly provide something to crow about! We crafted a plucky appliquéd apron to go along with this nutritious one-dish meal. The cover-up is easy to make by fusing fabric cutouts to a purchased apron.

NUTTY CHICKEN-BROCCOLI SALAD

   1   cup mayonnaise
 ¹/₄   cup sugar
   5   tablespoons raspberry vinegar
   2   cups cubed cooked chicken breast
   8   ounces bacon, cooked and
         crumbled
   4   cups small fresh broccoli
         flowerets (about 2 pounds)
 ¹/₂   cup dry-roasted cashews
 ¹/₂   cup sunflower kernels
 ¹/₂   cup chopped red onion
 ¹/₂   cup golden raisins

In a small bowl, combine mayonnaise, sugar, and vinegar; whisk dressing until well blended. In a large bowl, combine chicken, bacon, broccoli, cashews, sunflower kernels, onion, and raisins. Add dressing to chicken mixture; stir until well coated. Cover and chill 2 hours to let flavors blend. Store in an airtight container in refrigerator.

Yield: about 8 cups salad

ROOSTER APRON

You will need an apron, four coordinating fabrics (we used yellow, gold, red, and blue), paper-backed fusible web, assorted buttons, one small button for eye, and glue.

1. Use patterns, pages 114 and 115, and follow *Making Appliqués*, page 123, to make one *each* of rooster, straw, and sun

appliqués, five sun ray appliqués, and twelve track appliqués from fabrics.
2. Arrange appliqués on front of apron; fuse in place. Glue small button to rooster for eye.
3. Glue assorted buttons at top of bib and on apron front.

JUST "BEE-CAUSE!"

*S*urprise someone with a charming breakfast basket — just "bee-cause!" This sweet thinking-of-you gift features a pot of fruity Cherry Honey, packed with your oven-fresh biscuits. Made of honey and cherry preserves stirred together, the tasty spread provides a great start to a "buzz-y" day!

CHERRY HONEY

  1 jar (12 ounces) cherry preserves

¹/₂ cup honey

In a small bowl, combine preserves and honey; stir until well blended. Store in an airtight container in refrigerator.

Yield: about 1¹/₂ cups flavored honey

JUST "BEE-CAUSE!" BASKET AND GIFT TAG

You will need a basket with handle (we used a 9" dia. basket), bee-motif fabric for basket liner, 21" length of 2"w black and white grosgrain ribbon, artificial daisies and cherries, pinking shears, and glue.

For gift tag, you will *also* need a photocopy of tag design (page 119), yellow paper, black permanent felt-tip pen, serrated-edge craft scissors, and an artificial bee.

1. Use fabric and follow *Making a Basket Liner,* page 124, to make basket liner with pinked edges.

2. Glue daisies and cherries to basket handle. Tie ribbon into a bow around handle.

3. For gift tag, use craft scissors to cut out tag. Use pen to write message on tag. Glue tag to yellow paper. Leaving a ¹/₈" yellow border, cut out gift tag. Glue bee to corner of tag.

What better time than the chilly days of October to curl up in front of the television and enjoy our Crunchy Popcorn Mix! Toasted almonds and pecans make the crisp caramel corn even yummier. To delight a friend who loves popcorn, decoupage a bucket with magazine cutouts featuring popular TV stars.

CRUNCHY POPCORN MIX

16 cups popped popcorn
3 cups pecan halves, toasted
1 1/2 cups whole almonds, coarsely chopped and toasted
2 cups sugar
2 cups butter or margarine
1/2 cup light corn syrup
1/2 cup water
1 teaspoon salt
2 teaspoons vanilla extract

In a large greased roasting pan, combine popcorn, pecans, and almonds. Butter sides of a very heavy Dutch oven. Combine sugar, butter, corn syrup, water, and salt in pan. Stirring constantly, cook over medium-low heat until sugar dissolves. Using a pastry brush dipped in hot water, wash down any sugar crystals on sides of pan. Attach a candy thermometer to pan, making sure thermometer does not touch bottom of pan. Increase heat to medium and bring to a boil. Cook, without stirring, until mixture reaches soft-crack stage (approximately 270 to 290 degrees). Test about 1/2 teaspoon mixture in ice water. Mixture will form hard threads in ice water but will soften when removed from the water. Remove from heat and stir in vanilla. Pour over popcorn mixture; stir until well coated. Spread on greased aluminum foil. Use 2 greased forks to separate mixture into smaller pieces; allow to cool. Store in an airtight container.

Yield: about 25 cups popcorn mix

SHOWBIZ BUCKET

You will need a wedge-shaped galvanized bucket with handle (we used an 8 1/4" x 11 3/4" bucket), desired color spray paint, assorted motifs cut from magazines, 1 yd of 2 5/8"w wired ribbon, decoupage glue, clear acrylic spray sealer, foam brush, and wax paper.

1. Spray paint bucket; allow to dry.
2. Use foam brush to apply glue to wrong side of motifs. Glue motifs to outside of bucket, overlapping motifs as desired; allow to dry.
3. Allowing to dry between coats, apply two to three coats of sealer to bucket.
4. Tie ribbon into a bow around handle.
5. Line bucket with wax paper before placing food in bucket.

SHOWBIZ POPCORN

IRRESISTIBLE DESSERT BARS

*F*or *National Dessert Day (the second Thursday in October),* indulge your co-workers with irresistible Strawberry Cheesecake Bars! The fanciful tidbits are quickly prepared using a packaged mix and a few other simple ingredients. Our easy-to-paint glass plate makes a lovely showcase for these tasty treats.

STRAWBERRY CHEESECAKE BARS

  1 package (18¼ ounces) strawberry cake mix with pudding in the mix
  1 cup chopped pecans, toasted
  ¾ cup butter or margarine, melted
  2 packages (8 ounces each) cream cheese, softened
  1 cup sugar
  ⅓ cup strawberry jam

Preheat oven to 350 degrees. In a medium bowl, combine cake mix and pecans. Drizzle melted butter over mixture; stir until well blended. Press mixture into bottom of a greased 9 x 13-inch baking pan. In a medium bowl, beat cream cheese and sugar until smooth. Spread cream cheese mixture over crust. Process jam in a food processor until smooth. Spoon into a resealable plastic bag. Snip off 1 corner of bag. Pipe lengthwise lines of jam about 1 inch apart. Refer to Fig. 1 and use a knife to pull jam from side to side through cream cheese mixture at 1-inch intervals. Bake 18 to 23 minutes or until edges begin to brown and center is set. Cool in pan on a wire rack. Cover and chill 2 hours or until firm.

Fig. 1

Cut into 1 x 2-inch bars. Store in an airtight container in refrigerator.

Yield: about 4 dozen bars

PAINTED PLATE

You will need a 9" dia. clear glass plate, grease pencil, pink and dark pink Delta CeramDecor™ Air-Dry Perm enamel paint, paintbrushes, and a paper towel.

For gift tag, you will *also* need a photocopy of tag design (page 119) on pink parchment paper, pink construction paper, pink colored pencil, black permanent felt-tip pen, decorative-edge craft scissors, and glue.

1. Working on top of plate, use grease pencil to mark nineteen dots evenly around plate ¾" from edge. Draw a scallop between each dot. Add detail lines along each scallop.
2. Painting on bottom of plate only, use dark pink paint to paint dots and detail lines. Paint additional dots in center of plate as desired; allow to dry. Use pink paint to paint scallops.
3. Use paper towel to remove markings on top of plate.
4. Using supplies for gift tag, follow *Making a Tag*, page 122, to make gift tag.

SWEETEST DAY CANDIES

*W*ith only two simple ingredients, you can stir together these delightful tidbits to share with friends on Sweetest Day (the third Saturday in October). Nestled in individual candy cups and served on a pretty silver tray, Cookies and Cream Candies are elegant yet easy-to-make treats.

COOKIES AND CREAM CANDIES

  2 packages (12 ounces each)
      vanilla baking chips
26 chocolate sandwich cookies,
      coarsely chopped

Place about 5½ dozen paper candy cups on baking sheets. Melt baking chips in top of a double boiler over hot, not simmering, water. Reserving 3 tablespoons fine cookie crumbs to sprinkle on top of candies, fold remaining cookie pieces into melted baking chips. Drop rounded teaspoonfuls of mixture into candy cups. Sprinkle reserved cookie crumbs over candies before coating hardens. Chill about 15 minutes or until coating hardens. Store in an airtight container in a cool place.

Yield: about 5½ dozen candies

SWEETEST DAY GIFT TAG

You will need a photocopy of tag design (page 119), pink paper, pink colored pencil, black permanent felt-tip pen, decorative-edge craft scissors, and glue.

1. Use pink colored pencil to color tag design. Use pen to write message on tag. Cut out tag.
2. Glue tag to pink paper. Leaving a ¼" pink border, use craft scissors to cut out gift tag.

ORANGE SLICE FUDGE

Digging up something good to share on Halloween doesn't have to be a "grave" decision — just brew up a batch of microwave Orange Slice Fudge! Studded with pieces of a favorite candy, the creamy chocolates are presented in spray-painted tins that are simple to decorate with fun stickers. For frightfully easy finishes, tie the canisters with ribbon or glue on handmade labels.

ORANGE SLICE FUDGE

- ½ cup butter or margarine
- 3½ cups sifted confectioners sugar
- 1 can (5 ounces) evaporated milk
- ⅓ cup cocoa
- 1 package (11½ ounces) milk chocolate chips
- 1 package (10½ ounces) miniature marshmallows
- 2 teaspoons vanilla extract
- ¼ teaspoon salt
- 1 cup chopped orange slice candies

Line a 9 x 13-inch baking pan with aluminum foil; grease foil. Place butter in a large microwave-safe bowl; microwave on high power (100%) 1 minute or until butter melts. Stir in confectioners sugar, evaporated milk, and cocoa. Microwave on high power (100%) 4 minutes or until mixture comes to a boil, stirring every 2 minutes. Continue to microwave 4 minutes longer, stirring every 2 minutes. Add chocolate chips, marshmallows, vanilla, and salt; stir until well blended. Stir in candies. Pour into prepared pan. Refrigerate 4 hours or until firm. Cut into 1-inch squares, cleaning knife frequently.

Store in an airtight container in refrigerator.

Yield: about 8 dozen pieces fudge

GOBLIN COOKIES

*P*acked with flavor, *Jumbo Walnut-Chocolate Chunk Cookies are so good it's scary! When you serve these treats at your Halloween bash, your guests will be "goblin" them up. To make our easy edible "ghost," wrap a cookie in tissue paper, then use a felt-tip pen to draw a jack-o'-lantern face. A few ribbon streamers tie it all together.*

JUMBO WALNUT-CHOCOLATE CHUNK COOKIES

- 1 cup butter or margarine, melted
- 1 cup granulated sugar
- 1 cup firmly packed brown sugar
- 2 eggs
- 1 teaspoon vanilla-butter-nut flavoring
- 2 cups all-purpose flour
- 1 teaspoon baking powder
- 1 teaspoon baking soda
- 1/2 teaspoon salt
- 2 packages (10 ounces each) semisweet chocolate chunks
- 2 cups coarsely chopped walnuts

Preheat oven to 350 degrees. In a large bowl, beat butter and sugars until creamy. Add eggs and vanilla-butter-nut flavoring; beat until smooth. In a small bowl, combine flour, baking powder, baking soda, and salt. Add dry ingredients to creamed mixture; stir until a soft dough forms. Stir in chocolate chunks and walnuts. Use 1/4 cup of dough for each cookie. Drop cookies 3 inches apart onto a lightly greased baking sheet. Bake 12 to 15 minutes or until edges and tops are lightly browned. Transfer cookies to a wire rack to cool. Wrap cookies individually in plastic wrap.

Yield: about 2 1/2 dozen cookies

ORANGE POPCORN BALLS

*T*here's no trick to
scaring up these tasty treats!
Individually wrapped and
tied with curling ribbon,
our marshmallowy Orange
Popcorn Balls are quick,
yummy bites. The goblin
goodies are set out in a
spooky fabric-covered bag
so that trick-or-treaters
can grab their own — if
they dare!

ORANGE POPCORN BALLS

- 12 cups popped popcorn
- 6 tablespoons butter or margarine
- 3 cups miniature marshmallows
- 2 teaspoons orange extract
- 1 package (8.2 ounces) candy-
      coated peanut butter candy
      pieces

Place popcorn in a large bowl. In a
medium microwave-safe bowl, microwave
butter on high power (100%) 1 minute or
until melted. Add marshmallows.
Microwave 1 minute longer; stir until
melted. Stir in orange extract. Pour over
popcorn, stirring until well coated.
Sprinkle candies over coated popcorn;
stir just until candies are evenly
distributed. Allow popcorn to cool enough
to handle. Use lightly greased hands to
shape popcorn into 2-inch-diameter balls.
Place on waxed paper; cool completely.
Individually wrap popcorn balls.

Yield: about 16 popcorn balls

HALLOWEEN TREAT BAG

You will need a large paper grocery bag,
Halloween-motif fabric, paper-backed
fusible web, and four coordinating colors
of curling ribbon.
For tag, you will *also* need a photocopy of
tag design (page 119), orange paper,
purple marker, black permanent felt-tip
pen, hole punch, and glue.

1. Draw around front of bag on paper
side of web. Fuse web to wrong side of
fabric. Cut out along drawn lines. Fuse
fabric piece to front of bag.

2. Cut a sawtooth edge around top
of bag.

3. Tie several lengths of ribbon into a
bow around bag; curl ends.

4. For tag, use marker to color tag
design; cut out. Glue tag to orange
paper. Leaving a 1/8" orange border,
cut out tag. Use pen to write message
on tag. Punch hole in one corner of
tag. Tie tag to one ribbon end.

HALLOWEEN SNACK MIX

For a howling good time, treat Halloween tricksters to goody bags filled with our monster munchies! A kid-pleasing combination of three ready-to-eat ingredients, Halloween Snack Mix is a snap to toss together. The fun pumpkin bags are simple to create by decorating purchased gift sacks with hand-colored jack-o'-lanterns and ribbon bows.

HALLOWEEN SNACK MIX

  1 package (12¹/₂ ounces) candy corn
  1 package (12 ounces) chocolate-covered raisins
  1 container (5 ounces) puffed cheese ball snacks

In a large bowl, combine candy corn, raisins, and cheese snacks. Store in an airtight container in a cool place.

Yield: about 8 cups snack mix

PUMPKIN BAGS

For each bag, you will need a small black gift bag; white poster board; 8" length of ¹/₈"w ribbon; black permanent felt-tip marker; light orange, orange, and green colored pencils; small sharp scissors; tracing paper; transfer paper; and glue.

1. For *each* bag, trace pumpkin pattern, page 115, on tracing paper; cut out. Use transfer paper to transfer design on poster board. Using small scissors to cut out eyes, nose, and mouth, cut shape from poster board.
2. Use colored pencils to color pumpkin and stem.
3. Use marker to outline pumpkin, stem, eyes, nose, and mouth, and to draw detail lines.
4. Glue pumpkin to bag. Tie ribbon into a bow and glue to top of pumpkin.

There are some childhood things we never outgrow — like our love for peanut butter! Whether smooth and creamy or loaded with crunchy nuts, peanut butter is a spreadable dream. Declare your love for the gooey treat and your appreciation for a friend who shares your passion with a gift of Chocolate-Peanut Butter Candies. During Peanut Butter Lovers' Month (November), it's a sweet way to say, "I'm nuts about you!"

CHOCOLATE-PEANUT BUTTER CANDIES

1   package (12 ounces) semisweet chocolate chips
1   cup peanut butter chips
1   cup lightly salted peanuts
$^1/_2$ cup raisins

Place about 5 dozen paper candy cups on baking sheets. Melt chocolate chips and peanut butter chips in a heavy medium saucepan over low heat. Stir in peanuts and raisins. Drop teaspoonfuls of candy into candy cups. Chill 30 minutes or until candy is firm. Store in an airtight container in a cool place.

Yield: about 5 dozen candies

"I LOVE PEANUT BUTTER!" GIFT BOX

You will need a white gift box (we used a 3"w x 11"l x 3"h box), two coordinating fabrics, paper-backed fusible web, batting, gold paint pen, tracing paper, cardboard, and glue.

1. Use patterns, page 115, and follow *Making Appliqués*, page 123, to make one *each* of "I" and "!" appliqués from fabrics. Fuse to top of box.
2. Trace heart pattern, page 115, on tracing paper; cut out. Draw around pattern on cardboard, batting, and wrong side of fabric. Cut out cardboard and batting shapes along drawn lines. Cut out fabric shape $^1/_2$" outside drawn line. Clip curves of fabric shape to $^1/_8$" from drawn line.
3. Place batting heart on top of cardboard heart. Center fabric heart, right side up, over batting. Glue fabric edges to back of cardboard. Glue heart to box.
4. Use paint pen to draw around shapes, draw dots, and to write "Peanut Butter" on box.
5. Measure around sides of box; add $^1/_2$". Tear a 1"w fabric strip the determined measurement. Glue fabric strip around box.
6. For bow, tear a 1" x 12" fabric strip. Tie strip into a bow and glue to center front of box.

QUICK IRISH SODA BREAD

A gift of Irish Soda Bread Mix will delight a friend who loves to bake. Wrapped in cellophane and adorned with pretty trimmings, an ovenproof bread crock is the perfect gift container for this classic quick bread from the Emerald Isle. A matching gift tag announces your surprise and gives the simple baking instructions.

IRISH SODA BREAD MIX

- 3 cups all-purpose flour
- 3/4 cup quick-cooking oats
- 6 tablespoons dry buttermilk powder
- 1/4 cup sugar
- 1 teaspoon baking soda
- 1/2 teaspoon baking powder
- 1/2 teaspoon salt
- 2/3 cup chilled butter or margarine, cut into pieces
- 1 cup raisins

In a large bowl, combine flour, oats, buttermilk powder, sugar, baking soda, baking powder, and salt. Using a pastry blender or 2 knives, cut in chilled butter until mixture resembles coarse meal. Stir in raisins. Place mix in a resealable plastic bag. Store in refrigerator. Give with serving instructions.

Yield: about 6½ cups bread mix (makes 1 loaf bread)

To serve: Store bread mix in refrigerator until ready to prepare. Preheat oven to 350 degrees. In a medium bowl, combine bread mix and 1½ cups water; stir just until a soft dough forms. Spoon dough into a greased 1½-quart ovenproof bread crock or a 5 x 9-inch loaf pan. Smooth

top of dough. Bake 1 to 1¼ hours or until top is browned and a wooden skewer inserted in center of bread comes out clean. Cool in crock 10 minutes. Remove from crock and serve warm or transfer to a wire rack to cool completely. Store in an airtight container.

BREAD CROCK AND TAG

You will need a 1½-quart ovenproof bread crock, resealable plastic bag, cellophane, 26" length of 1¼"w ribbon, several 26" lengths of raffia, three artificial sunflowers with leaves, and glue. *For gift tag,* you will *also* need a photocopy of tag design (page 119) on parchment paper, brown handmade

paper, decorative-edge craft scissors, and a black permanent felt-tip pen.

1. Place bread mix in plastic bag; place bag in crock.
2. Wrap cellophane around crock, gathering edges at top. Tie ribbon and raffia into a bow around gathers to secure. Glue two flowers to knot of bow.
3. For gift tag, leaving a 1/8" border around design, cut out tag. Glue tag to brown paper. Leaving a 1/2" brown border, use craft scissors to cut out gift tag.
4. Use pen to write mixing and baking instructions on tag. Glue remaining flower to tag.
5. Store in refrigerator.

PUMPKIN COOKIE HARVEST

*F*riends and neighbors
will give thanks for a harvest
of pretty Pumpkin Cookies.
The lightly spiced treats are
flavored with orange and
decorated with icing. A
pumpkin-shaped wire basket
makes a fitting carrier.

PUMPKIN COOKIES

COOKIES

1¹⁄₂	cups butter or margarine, softened
1	cup sugar
2	eggs
1¹⁄₂	teaspoons orange extract
1	teaspoon vanilla extract
¹⁄₈	teaspoon orange paste food coloring
3¹⁄₂	cups all-purpose flour
1¹⁄₄	teaspoons baking powder
1	teaspoon pumpkin pie spice
¹⁄₂	teaspoon salt

ICING

1	ounce semisweet baking chocolate
2	tablespoons milk
1	tablespoon butter or margarine
1¹⁄₄	cups sifted confectioners sugar
³⁄₄	teaspoon vanilla extract
¹⁄₄	teaspoon orange extract
1	tube (4¹⁄₄ ounces) green decorating icing

For cookies, cream butter and sugar in a large bowl until fluffy. Add eggs, extracts, and food coloring; beat until smooth. In a medium bowl, combine flour, baking powder, pumpkin pie spice, and salt. Add dry ingredients to creamed mixture; stir until a soft dough forms. Divide dough into fourths. Wrap in plastic wrap and chill 2 hours or until dough is firm enough to handle.

Preheat oven to 375 degrees. On a lightly floured surface, use a floured rolling pin to roll out one fourth of dough to ¹⁄₄-inch thickness. Use a 4-inch-wide pumpkin-shaped cookie cutter to cut out cookies. Transfer to a lightly greased baking sheet. Bake 7 to 9 minutes or until bottoms are lightly browned. Transfer cookies to a wire rack to cool.

For icing, combine chocolate, milk, and butter in a small microwave-safe bowl. Microwave on high power (100%) 1 minute, stirring every 30 seconds until chocolate softens; stir until smooth. Cool chocolate mixture 10 minutes. Add confectioners sugar and extracts; beat until well blended. Spoon chocolate icing into a pastry bag fitted with a small round tip; pipe outline and curved lines onto cookies. Fill in stem with chocolate icing. Transfer green icing into a pastry bag fitted with a small round tip; pipe vines onto cookies. Use green icing and a medium leaf tip to pipe leaves onto cookies. Allow icing to harden. Store in an airtight container in a single layer.

Yield: about 2 dozen cookies

Autumn's bounty is richly displayed on these gorgeous bags. Both feature cutout "windows" and colorful ribbons and leaves. Pack the bags with our spiced popcorn mix, which is glazed with brown sugar and molasses. The recipe makes plenty for several gifts.

AUTUMN POPCORN MIX

24 cups popped popcorn
 2 cups walnut halves
 1 cup butter or margarine
 2 cups firmly packed brown sugar
 1/2 cup molasses
 1 teaspoon salt
 1 teaspoon vanilla extract
 1 teaspoon apple pie spice
 1/2 teaspoon baking soda
 2 packages (12 1/2 ounces each)
      candy corn

Preheat oven to 250 degrees. Combine popcorn and walnuts in a lightly greased large roasting pan. In a heavy large saucepan, melt butter over medium-high heat. Stir in brown sugar, molasses, and salt. Stirring constantly, bring mixture to a boil. Boil 5 minutes without stirring.

Remove from heat; stir in vanilla, apple pie spice, and baking soda (mixture will foam). Pour syrup over popcorn mixture; stir until well coated. Bake 1 hour, stirring every 15 minutes. Spread on lightly greased aluminum foil to cool. Sprinkle candy corn over popcorn mixture. Store in an airtight container.

Yield: about 30 cups popcorn mix

LEAF CUTOUT BAG

You will need a brown lunch bag, 2 yds of 5/8"w wired ribbon, clear cellophane, tissue paper, tracing paper, hole punch, small sharp scissors, and glue.

1. Trace leaf pattern, page 116, onto tracing paper; cut out. Draw around pattern on bag. Use scissors to carefully cut out leaf.
2. Cut a piece of cellophane 1/2" larger on all sides than pattern. Center cellophane over leaf opening on inside of bag; glue in place.
3. Line bag with tissue paper. Place gift in bag.
4. Fold top of bag 1 3/4" to back. Punch two holes 2" apart in folded part of bag. Cut one 16" and two 28" lengths of ribbon. Thread short ribbon length through holes in bag and knot at front. Tie long ribbon lengths together into a bow around knot. Arrange bow and streamers on front of bag.

AUTUMN WINDOW BAG

You will need a 4" x 7 1/2" x 12h" corrugated cardboard gift bag, fabric for border of window, paper-backed fusible web, tracing paper, clear cellophane, poster board, craft knife and piece of cardboard to fit inside bag, yellow and orange curling ribbon, 1 yd of 1/4"w brown satin ribbon, artificial autumn leaves on stems, and glue.

For gift tag, you will *also* need brown paper, kraft paper, brown permanent felt-tip pen, and a hole punch.

1. For window, trace arch patterns, page 116, separately onto tracing paper; cut out.
2. Center large arch pattern on front of bag and use a pencil to draw around pattern. Place cardboard in bag and use craft knife to cut opening in bag for window.
3. Cut a piece of poster board, web, fabric, and cellophane same width and 1" shorter than front of bag. Fuse fabric to poster board. Draw around small arch pattern at center on wrong side of fabric-covered poster board. Use craft knife to cut opening in poster board. Center cellophane over opening on fabric side of poster board; glue in place. Centering poster board opening in window of bag, glue fabric-covered poster board to inside of bag.
4. Glue one stem of leaves at bottom of window.
5. Cut several lengths of each color curling ribbon. Use curling and satin ribbons to tie a multi-loop bow. Curl streamers of curling ribbon. Glue bow at top of window. Arrange streamers as desired; glue in place. Glue leaves to bow and streamers.
6. For gift tag, tear a 1 3/4" x 2 1/2" piece of kraft paper and a 2 1/4" x 3" piece of brown paper. Center and glue kraft paper piece to brown paper piece. Use pen to write message on tag. Punch hole in tag. Tie tag to end of one streamer.

HAPPY BIRTHDAY KIT

*S*how a friend the bright side of turning a year older with a fun-filled birthday kit! The bag is packed with everything the honoree will need to have a happy day, including our oh-so-good Fudgy Chocolate Chip Cupcakes! Baked with three kinds of chocolate, these moist, densely rich "sin-sations" are created especially for the adult chocoholic. Delivered on a festively wrapped fabric-covered tray, these treats are one of the sweet rewards of getting older.

FUDGY CHOCOLATE CHIP CUPCAKES

CUPCAKES
3/4 cup butter or margarine, softened
1/2 cup sugar
3 eggs
1 teaspoon vanilla extract
3/4 cup plus 2 tablespoons all-purpose flour
1/2 teaspoon baking soda
1/4 teaspoon salt
3/4 cup buttermilk
12 ounces semisweet baking chocolate, melted
1 package (12 ounces) semisweet chocolate mini chips

ICING
2 cups sugar
1/4 cup cocoa
1/2 cup butter or margarine
1/2 cup milk
1 tablespoon light corn syrup
1 teaspoon vanilla extract

Preheat oven to 350 degrees. For cupcakes, cream butter and sugar in a large bowl until fluffy. Add eggs and vanilla; beat until well blended. In a small bowl, combine flour, baking soda, and salt. Alternately add dry ingredients, buttermilk, and melted chocolate to creamed mixture; beat until well blended. Stir in chocolate chips. Spoon batter into paper-lined muffin cups. Bake 18 to 22 minutes or until a toothpick inserted near center of cupcake comes out with a few crumbs clinging to it. Cool in pan 10 minutes; transfer cupcakes to a wire rack to cool completely.

For icing, combine sugar and cocoa in a medium saucepan. Add butter, milk, and corn syrup. Stirring constantly, bring to a boil over medium heat; boil 2 minutes. Transfer icing to a medium heat-resistant bowl; cool 5 minutes. Add vanilla. Place icing over a bowl of ice and beat with electric mixer about 5 minutes or until icing is thick enough to spread. Ice cupcakes, using about 1 tablespoon icing for each cupcake. Allow icing to harden. Store in an airtight container in a cool place.

Yield: about 2 dozen cupcakes

BIRTHDAY KIT

You will need a shoe box lid, fabric, large brown paper grocery bag, paper-backed fusible web, assorted colors of curling ribbon, party supplies (we used hats, noisemakers, balloons, plates, and napkins), cellophane, and glue.
For label, you will *also* need blue and yellow construction paper and a red permanent felt-tip marker.

1. For cupcake tray, measure length and width of shoe box lid, including inside and outside of each side (Fig. 1). Add 1" to each measurement. Cut a piece of fabric the determined measurements.

Fig. 1

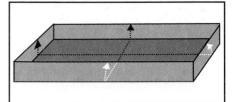

2. Center lid, top side down, on wrong side of fabric piece. Folding fabric to inside of box and pleating corners as necessary, glue edges of fabric piece to lid to secure.
3. For bottom of container, draw around bottom of lid onto wrong side of fabric. Cutting 1/4" inside drawn lines, cut out shape. Glue fabric piece to bottom of container.
4. Place cupcakes on tray. Wrap cellophane around tray, gathering edges at top. Tie several lengths of curling ribbon into a bow around gathers to secure; curl ribbon ends.
5. Draw around front of bag on paper side of web. Fuse web to wrong side of fabric. Cut out along drawn lines. Fuse fabric piece to front of bag. Fold top of bag 3 1/4" to the outside.
6. For label, cut a 3 1/2" x 11 1/2" piece from blue construction paper and a 2 1/2" x 9" piece from yellow construction paper. Use marker to write message on yellow paper. Center and glue yellow paper to blue paper. Glue label to top front of bag.
7. Glue curling ribbon lengths to inside of one hat; curl ends. Glue hat to label. Glue one noisemaker to label. Place remaining party supplies in bag.

*H*elp a friend through the hectic holiday shopping season with our clever survival kit! Apricot Cider is a delicious way to unwind after a long day at the mall, and it's great whether served warm or over ice. You'll also want to include a few shopping "necessities" such as a notepad, emergency snacks, and pain relievers. For a quick, festive finish, tie on a seasonal bow and a handmade tag.

APRICOT CIDER

2   quarts apple cider
2   cans (11¹/₂ ounces each) apricot nectar
2   cups apricot brandy
1   tablespoon freshly squeezed lemon juice

In a 1-gallon container, combine apple cider, apricot nectar, apricot brandy, and lemon juice. Store in an airtight container in refrigerator. Serve warm or over ice with a lemon slice.

Yield: about 12¹/₂ cups apricot cider

CHRISTMAS SHOPPER GIFT TAG

You will need a photocopy of tag design (page 119), green paper, red marker, decorative-edge craft scissors, black permanent felt-tip pen, and glue.

1. Use red marker to color tag design. Use pen to write message on tag. Cut out tag.
2. Glue tag to green paper. Leaving a ¹/₄" green border, use craft scissors to cut out gift tag.

Only 24 shopping
days 'til Xmas!

WARM WINTER WELCOME

*W*elcome winter by sharing cups of steaming Strawberry-Vanilla Drink and a bit of warm conversation with your friends. The recipe yields lots of mix, so you can pack some in wintry snowman jars for gift-giving. A jaunty hat and cozy scarf lend charm to the frosty project, which begins with a "recycled" food jar.

STRAWBERRY-VANILLA DRINK MIX

- 1 package (25.6 ounces) nonfat dry milk powder
- 1 package (16 ounces) strawberry-flavored confectioners sugar, sifted
- 2 jars (8 ounces each) French vanilla-flavored non-dairy powdered creamer
- 1 package (16 ounces) strawberry mix for milk
- 1 jar (11 ounces) non-dairy powdered creamer
- 1/2 teaspoon salt

In a very large bowl, combine all ingredients; stir until well blended. Store in an airtight container. Give with serving instructions.

Yield: about 20 cups drink mix

To serve: For a hot drink, pour 6 ounces hot water over 3 heaping tablespoons drink mix; stir until well blended.

For a cold strawberry-vanilla shake, place 6 ounces cold water, 3 heaping tablespoons drink mix, and 1 to 2 scoops vanilla ice cream in a blender. Blend until desired consistency.

SNOWMAN JAR

You will need an empty 32-ounce mayonnaise jar with lid, a 2¹/₂" dia. plastic foam ball, paring knife, snow texturing medium, small flat paintbrush, 5" x 18" fabric strip, black felt, 3" length of orange paper twist (untwisted), six straight pins with black heads, two 6" long twigs, 4" dia. black felt hat, 1³/₄" dia. artificial sunflower, Spanish moss, artificial bird, three ³/₄" dia. black buttons, and glue.

1. Use knife to cut ¹/₄" from one side of ball, forming a flat surface (bottom). Glue bottom of ball to top of jar lid.

2. Use paintbrush to apply snow texturing medium to ball; allow to dry.

3. For nose, cut a 1" x 3" length from paper twist. Roll paper twist into a 1" long cone shape. Use a pencil to make a small indentation at center of snow-covered ball for nose. Glue nose to head.

4. For eyes, cut two ¹/₄" dia. circles from felt. Glue eyes to head.

5. Insert pins into head for mouth.

6. For arms, glue twigs to jar lid.

7. For scarf, tie fabric strip around bottom of ball.

8. Form moss into a nest shape; glue nest and bird to top of hat. Glue flower to front of hat. Glue hat to top of head.

9. Glue buttons to front of jar.

HANUKKAH TRADITION

A sumptuous
*Hanukkah surprise, our
Apricot-Walnut Rugelach
features a spicy fruit filling
rolled in rich cream cheese
pastry. The crescent-shaped
cookies are a traditional
holiday favorite, and they
make an especially thoughtful
gift when presented in a pretty
container. Embellished with the
Star of David, the painted box is
simply tied with a silver ribbon.*

APRICOT-WALNUT RUGELACH

DOUGH

  1 package (8 ounces) cream cheese,
     softened
  ³/₄ cup butter or margarine, softened
  2 tablespoons sugar
  1 teaspoon almond extract
  1¹/₂ cups all-purpose flour

FILLING

  ³/₄ cup golden raisins
  ¹/₄ cup firmly packed brown sugar
  2 tablespoons granulated sugar
  1 teaspoon ground cinnamon
  ¹/₄ teaspoon ground cardamom
  1 cup chopped walnuts, toasted
  3 tablespoons butter or margarine,
     softened and divided
  6 tablespoons apricot preserves,
     divided

For dough, beat cream cheese, butter,
sugar, and almond extract in a medium
bowl until fluffy. Add flour; stir until a soft
dough forms. Divide dough into 3 balls.
Wrap in plastic wrap and chill overnight.

Preheat oven to 350 degrees. For
filling, process raisins, sugars, cinnamon,
and cardamom in a food processor until
raisins are coarsely chopped. Add walnuts
and continue to process until walnuts are
finely chopped. On a heavily floured
surface, use a floured rolling pin to roll
1 ball of dough into a 12-inch-diameter
circle. Spread 1 tablespoon butter over
dough circle. Spread 2 tablespoons
preserves over buttered dough circle.
Sprinkle about 8 tablespoons filling over
dough. Use a pizza cutter to cut dough
into quarters; cut each quarter into
3 equal wedges of dough. Beginning at
wide end, roll up each wedge. Transfer to
a baking sheet lined with parchment
paper. Repeat with remaining dough and
filling. Bake 15 to 20 minutes or until
edges are lightly browned. Transfer
cookies to a wire rack to cool. Store in
an airtight container.

Yield: 3 dozen cookies

HANUKKAH BOX

You will need an 8¹/₂" hexagon-shaped
papier-mâché box with lid, blue spray
paint, silver acrylic paint, paintbrush,
tracing paper, transfer paper, and 42"
length of 2"w silver-beaded ribbon.

1. Spray paint box blue; allow to dry.
2. Trace star pattern, page 117, on tracing
paper. Use transfer paper to transfer
design to top of box lid.
3. Paint star design silver; allow to dry.
4. Place gift in box. Replace lid.
5. Knot ribbon around box.

GOLDEN PEAR HONEY

*O*ur golden Pear
Honey makes a pleasing
gift for almost anyone on
your Christmas list. Naturally
delicious, the fruity spread
blends fresh pears with the
tropical flavor of pineapple.
To present this irresistible
treat, nestle a ribbon-tied jar
of honey in a bag that you
stamp with a pear motif. The
motif, created with a real pear,
is repeated on the gift card and
accented with silk leaves.

PEAR HONEY

    7   cups peeled, cored, and chopped
          ripe pears (about 8 pears)
    4   cups sugar
    1   can (15¹/₄ ounces) crushed
          pineapple in juice, drained

Process pears in a food processor until
finely chopped. Combine pears and sugar
in a heavy Dutch oven. Stirring frequently,
bring mixture to a boil over medium heat
and cook until sugar dissolves. Reduce
heat to low. Stirring occasionally, simmer
about 45 minutes or until mixture
thickens. Add pineapple; cook 5 minutes
longer. Spoon mixture into heat-resistant
jars; cover and cool to room temperature.
Store in refrigerator.

Yield: about 6 cups pear honey

STAMPED BAG AND CARD

You will need a 6"h gift bag, 5" x 7" note
card with matching envelope (we used a
card and envelope with a red deckle
edge), pear with stem, gold acrylic paint,
gold paint pen, silk leaves, paper towel,
ruler, and glue.

1. Remove stem and cut pear in half
vertically.

2. Use one pear half and stem and follow
Sponge Painting, page 123, to stamp
gold pear and stem shapes on bag.
3. Glue leaf to bag.
4. Repeat Steps 2 and 3 to stamp pear on
note card.
5. Use paint pen and ruler to draw lines
and dots along edge of card.

102

HEAVENLY LITTLE CAKES

As a gesture of goodwill, share our tasty little Orange Slice Cakes with friends who've been angels to you. Each loaf is wrapped in cellophane, tied with golden ribbon, and adorned with a cherub sticker to make heavenly treats for the holiday season.

ORANGE SLICE CAKES

- 1 package (18 ounces) orange slice gumdrop candies
- 2 cups chopped walnuts
- 1 package (8 ounces) chopped dates
- 1 can (3$^{1}/_{2}$ ounces) flaked coconut
- 3$^{1}/_{4}$ cups all-purpose flour, divided
- 1 teaspoon baking soda
- $^{1}/_{2}$ teaspoon salt
- 1 cup butter or margarine, softened
- 1$^{1}/_{2}$ cups granulated sugar
- $^{1}/_{2}$ cup firmly packed brown sugar
- 4 eggs
- 1 teaspoon vanilla extract
- 1 cup buttermilk
- $^{3}/_{4}$ cup sifted confectioners sugar
- $^{1}/_{3}$ cup orange juice
- 1 teaspoon grated orange zest

Preheat oven to 300 degrees. Line 2$^{1}/_{2}$ x 4-inch loaf pans with aluminum foil loaf baking cups. Reserve 7 candies; chop remaining candies. On a sugared surface, use a rolling pin to roll out reserved candies to $^{1}/_{8}$-inch thickness. Cut out "petals" using a teardrop-shaped aspic cutter; set aside.

In a medium bowl, combine chopped candies, walnuts, dates, and coconut. Add $^{1}/_{2}$ cup flour; stir until mixture is coated. In another medium bowl, combine remaining 2$^{3}/_{4}$ cups flour, baking soda, and salt. In a large bowl, cream butter, granulated sugar, and brown sugar until fluffy. Add eggs and vanilla; beat until smooth. Alternately beat dry ingredients and buttermilk into creamed mixture, beating until well blended. Stir in fruit and nut mixture. Spoon batter into prepared pans. Place 5 candy petals on each cake. Bake 45 to 55 minutes or until a toothpick inserted in center of cake comes out clean.

In a small bowl, combine confectioners sugar, orange juice, and orange zest; whisk until smooth. Use a wooden skewer to poke holes about 1 inch apart in top of each warm cake. Spoon about 1 teaspoon glaze over each cake. Store in an airtight container.

Yield: about 18 small cakes

*F*estive shapes and the tempting aroma of cinnamon make our Spicy Christmas Tree Cookies a gift that an entire family can enjoy! For sharing, the iced treats are packed in a fabric-covered box embellished with ribbon and a paper tree.

SPICY CHRISTMAS TREE COOKIES

COOKIES
- $2/3$ cup firmly packed brown sugar
- $2/3$ cup molasses
- $3/4$ cup butter or margarine
- 1 egg
- 1 teaspoon orange extract
- $3^1/2$ cups all-purpose flour
- 2 teaspoons ground cinnamon
- $1/2$ teaspoon ground cardamom
- $1/2$ teaspoon baking soda

ICING
- $1^1/2$ cups sifted confectioners sugar
- 1 to 2 tablespoons water
- $1/2$ teaspoon vanilla extract
- $1/4$ to $1/2$ teaspoon red paste food coloring

For cookies, combine brown sugar and molasses in a heavy small saucepan. Stirring constantly, cook over medium-high heat until mixture boils. Boil 1 minute; remove from heat. In a large bowl, combine butter and hot sugar mixture; stir until butter melts. Add egg and orange extract; beat until well blended. In a medium bowl, combine flour, cinnamon, cardamom, and baking soda. Add dry ingredients to butter mixture; stir until well blended. Divide dough into thirds. Wrap in plastic wrap and chill 2 hours.

Preheat oven to 350 degrees. On a lightly floured surface, use a floured rolling pin to roll out one third of dough into a 9-inch-high x 14-inch-wide rectangle. Make 3-inch-wide lengthwise cuts with a knife. Use a scalloped-edged pastry cutter to make a diagonal cut from upper left corner to $4^1/8$ inches from lower left corner (Fig. 1).

Fig. 1

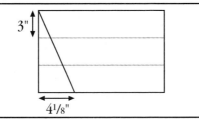

Make a second diagonal cut $2^3/4$ inches from first cut (Fig. 2).

Fig. 2

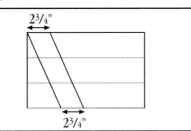

Continue making diagonal cuts $2^3/4$ inches from previous cuts. Refer to Fig. 3 to make a diagonal cut $2^3/4$ inches from upper left corner to lower lengthwise cut.

Fig. 3

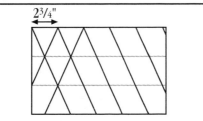

Continue to make diagonal cuts $2^3/4$ inches from previous cuts to form triangles. Transfer to a lightly greased baking sheet. Bake 5 to 7 minutes or until edges are lightly browned. Transfer

cookies to a wire rack to cool. Repeat with remaining dough.

For icing, combine confectioners sugar, water, and vanilla in a small bowl; stir until smooth. Tint red. Spoon icing into a pastry bag fitted with a small round tip. Pipe design onto cookies. Allow icing to harden. Store in an airtight container.

Yield: about $6^1/2$ dozen cookies

CHRISTMAS TREE BOX

You will need a $10^3/4$" dia. papier-mâché box with lid, three coordinating fabrics, paper-backed fusible web, 2 yds of $3/8$"w and 1 yd of $7/8$"w ribbon, red dimensional paint, 7" square of kraft paper, and glue.

1. Use patterns, page 118, and follow *Making Appliqués*, page 123, to make one large tree appliqué from one fabric, one medium tree appliqué from another fabric, and one small tree appliqué from kraft paper.
2. Trace around lid on paper side of web. Cutting $1/2$" outside drawn line, cut out web shape. Fuse to wrong side of remaining fabric. Cut out along drawn line; fuse to top of lid.
3. Layering shapes from largest to smallest, center and fuse tree appliqués to lid.
4. Use red paint to paint design down center of small tree.
5. For bow, cut two 17" lengths from $3/8$"w ribbon. Tie ribbon lengths together into a bow. Glue bow to bottom of tree.
6. For ribbon trims, measure around lid and box; add $1/2$" to each measurement. Cut a length from each ribbon the determined measurements. Overlapping ends, glue ribbon lengths around sides of lid and box.

BLACK WALNUT BRITTLE

*T*his country-style stocking is so cute even Santa will want one — especially since we filled it with crunchy Black Walnut Brittle! A plain canvas stocking is easily embellished with fused-on fabric, buttons, and pen "stitches" to create the charming holder.

BLACK WALNUT BRITTLE

2 cups sugar
1/2 cup light corn syrup
1/3 cup water
1/4 teaspoon salt
1 cup chopped black walnuts
3 tablespoons butter or margarine
1 teaspoon vanilla extract
1 teaspoon baking soda

Butter sides of a heavy large saucepan. Combine sugar, corn syrup, water, and salt in saucepan. Stirring constantly, cook over medium-low heat until sugar dissolves. Using a pastry brush dipped in hot water, wash down any sugar crystals on sides of pan. Attach a candy thermometer to pan, making sure thermometer does not touch bottom of pan. Increase heat to medium and bring to a boil. Cook, without stirring, about 10 minutes or until mixture reaches 260 degrees. Stir in walnuts and continue cooking until mixture reaches hard-crack stage (approximately 300 to 310 degrees). Test about 1/2 teaspoon mixture in ice water. Mixture will form brittle threads in ice water and will remain brittle when removed from the water. Remove from heat and add butter and vanilla; stir until butter melts. Stir in baking soda (mixture will foam). Pour candy onto a large piece of greased aluminum foil placed on a dampened flat surface. Using 2 greased wooden spoons, pull warm candy until stretched thin. Cool completely. Break into pieces. Store in an airtight container.

Yield: about 1 1/2 pounds candy

CANVAS CHRISTMAS STOCKING

You will need a 14"h canvas stocking, three coordinating fabrics, 1 1/2" x 18" torn fabric strip for bow, paper-backed fusible web, three 1" dia. buttons, one 3/4" dia. button, black permanent felt-tip pen, pinking shears, and glue.

1. Place stocking, wrong side up, on paper side of web. Draw around stocking. Leaving a 1/8" border, cut toe, heel, and cuff shapes from drawn stocking on web. Fuse shapes to desired fabrics; cut out. Fuse toe and heel to stocking.
2. Use pinking shears to trim top and bottom edges of cuff. Fuse cuff to stocking.
3. Use pen to draw three H's on front of stocking and "stitches" along outside edges of heel, toe, and cuff. Glue one 1" dia. button beside each H.
4. Tie fabric strip into a bow and glue to cuff; fringe ends. Glue remaining button to knot of bow.

SANTA'S SWEETSHOP PRETZELS

A visit to Santa's
sweetshop inspired our
tempting Toffee-Sprinkled
Pretzels. The crunchy
chocolate-dipped morsels
are ideal for holiday snacking,
and even better for holiday
sharing! Adorned with a pretty
cross-stitched wreath and a
simple Christmas message,
our mini tote helps make
your gift especially sweet.

TOFFEE-SPRINKLED PRETZELS

1 package (7¹/₂ ounces) almond
    brickle chips
12 ounces chocolate candy coating,
    chopped
1¹/₂ cups semisweet chocolate chips
1 package (10 ounces) small pretzel
    twists

Pulse process brickle chips in a food
processor until finely chopped; set aside.
Melt candy coating and chocolate chips in
a heavy medium saucepan over low heat.
Remove from heat (if chocolate begins to
harden, return to heat). Drop several
pretzels at a time into chocolate, stirring
to coat. Transfer pretzels to a baking sheet
lined with waxed paper. Before chocolate
hardens, sprinkle brickle pieces over
pretzels. Chill 2 hours or until chocolate
hardens. Store in an airtight container in
a cool place.

Yield: about 17 dozen pretzels

CHRISTMAS TOTE

You will need a 4¹/₂" x 6¹/₂" Aida tote
bag (14 ct) and embroidery floss (see
color key, page 118).

Using three strands of floss for Cross
Stitch and one strand of floss for
Backstitch, follow *Cross Stitch*, page 124,
to center and stitch wreath design,
page 118, on tote.

PATTERNS

SNOWFLAKE PLACE MATS AND
JAR LID COVER

(Page 6)

C

A

B

PAINTED PEPPERS
CONTAINER

(Page 11)

108

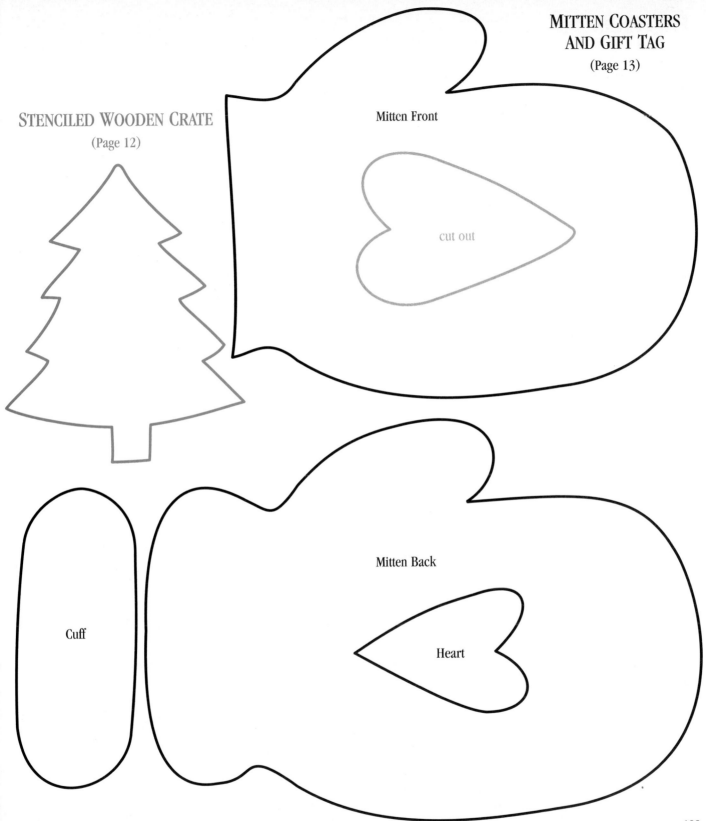

STENCILED WOODEN CRATE
(Page 12)

MITTEN COASTERS
AND GIFT TAG
(Page 13)

Mitten Front

cut out

Mitten Back

Cuff

Heart

109

PATTERNS (continued)

PAINTED CHERRY TINS
(Page 16)

COOKIE CRAYON BOX
(Page 24)

TOUCHDOWN BASKET
(Page 15)

BIRDHOUSE COOKIES
(Page 22)

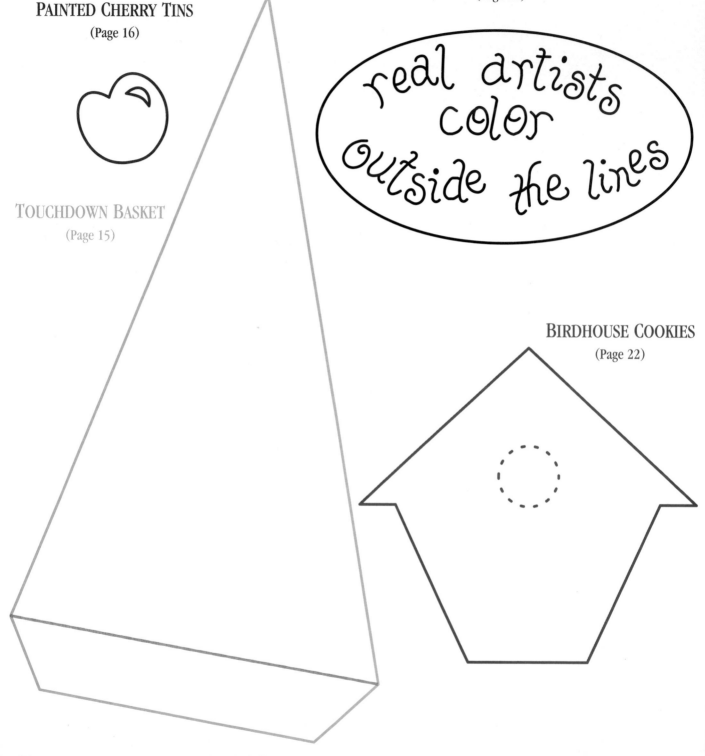

real artists color outside the lines

GOOF-OFF DAY FLAG
(Page 29)

BUNNY TREATS JAR
(Page 38)

PAINTED SALAD BOWL
(Page 40)

PATTERNS (continued)

CINCO DE MAYO BASKET
(Page 44)

A

B

DAD'S DAY SHIRT BOX
(Page 55)

FLAG PLATE
(Page 64)

Easy Hot Dog Relish

PICNIC BASKET

(Page 58)

WATERMELON POT
AND JAR LID

(Page 69)

RADISH BASKET

(Page 72)

CROSS-STITCH JAR LID

(Page 76)

GREAT NEIGHBOR GIFT BOX AND TAG

(Page 79)

Thanks
for being a
great
Neighbor

the
thought!

Relish the Thought! (26w x 23h)

X	DMC	B'ST	ANC.	COLOR
	469	✓	267	dk green
▲	471		266	green
	666	✓	46	red
⊡	666	French Knot		

PATTERNS (continued)

ROOSTER APRON

(Page 80)

Sun Ray
(cut 5)

Rooster

Track

Straw

Sun

PUMPKIN BAGS
(Page 89)

"I LOVE PEANUT BUTTER!"
GIFT BOX
(Page 90)

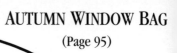

LEAF CUTOUT BAG

(Page 95)

Large Arch

Small Arch

Leaf

HANUKKAH BOX
(Page 101)

PATTERNS (continued)

CHRISTMAS TOTE
(Page 107)

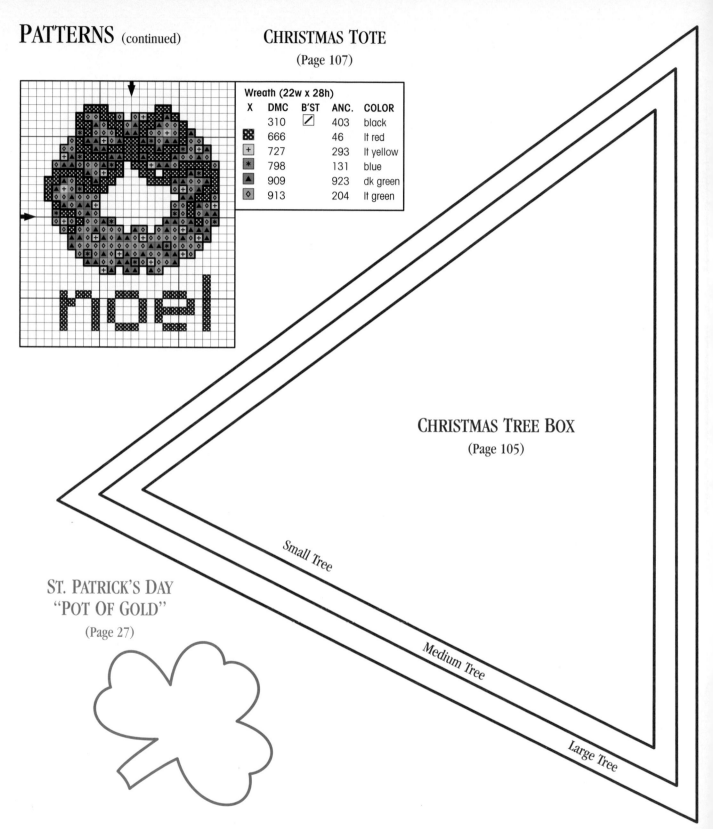

Wreath (22w x 28h)

X	DMC	B'ST	ANC.	COLOR
	310	╱	403	black
▨	666		46	lt red
+	727		293	lt yellow
✳	798		131	blue
▲	909		923	dk green
◇	913		204	lt green

CHRISTMAS TREE BOX
(Page 105)

Small Tree

Medium Tree

Large Tree

ST. PATRICK'S DAY "POT OF GOLD"
(Page 27)

TAG DESIGNS

To:
From:

"SWEET DREAMS!"
GIFT TAG
(Page 48)

KITCHEN TIPS

MEASURING INGREDIENTS

Liquid measuring cups have a rim above the measuring line to keep liquid ingredients from spilling. Nested measuring cups are used to measure dry ingredients, butter, shortening, and peanut butter. Measuring spoons are used for measuring both dry and liquid ingredients.

To measure flour or granulated sugar: Spoon ingredient into nested measuring cup and level off with a knife. Do not pack down with spoon.

To measure confectioners sugar: Sift sugar, spoon lightly into nested measuring cup, and level off with a knife.

To measure brown sugar: Pack sugar into nested measuring cup and level off with a knife. Sugar should hold its shape when removed from cup.

To measure dry ingredients equaling less than 1/4 cup: Dip measuring spoon into ingredient and level off with a knife.

To measure butter, shortening, or peanut butter: Pack ingredient firmly into nested measuring cup and level off with a knife.

To measure liquids: Use a liquid measuring cup placed on a flat surface. Pour ingredient into cup and check measuring line at eye level.

To measure honey or syrup: For a more accurate measurement, lightly spray measuring cup or spoon with cooking spray before measuring so the liquid will release easily from cup or spoon.

SOFTENING BUTTER OR MARGARINE

To soften 1 stick of butter, remove wrapper and place butter on a microwave-safe plate. Microwave on medium-low power (30%) 20 to 30 seconds.

SOFTENING CREAM CHEESE

To soften cream cheese, remove wrapper and place cream cheese on a microwave-safe plate. Microwave on medium power (50%) 1 to 1 1/2 minutes for an 8-ounce package or 30 to 45 seconds for a 3-ounce package.

SHREDDING CHEESE

To shred cheese easily, place wrapped cheese in freezer 10 to 20 minutes before shredding.

TOASTING NUTS

To toast nuts, spread nuts on an ungreased baking sheet. Stirring occasionally, bake in a 350-degree oven 5 to 8 minutes or until nuts are slightly darker in color.

PREPARING CITRUS FRUIT ZEST

To remove the zest (colored outer portion of peel) from citrus fruits, use a fine grater or fruit zester, being careful not to grate white portion of peel, which is bitter.

WHIPPING CREAM

For greatest volume, chill a glass bowl, beaters, and cream before whipping. In warm weather, place chilled bowl over ice while whipping cream.

SUBSTITUTING HERBS

To substitute fresh herbs for dried, use 1 tablespoon fresh chopped herbs for 1/2 teaspoon dried herbs.

CUTTING OUT COOKIES

Place a piece of white paper over pattern (for a more durable pattern, use stencil plastic which is available at craft stores). Use a permanent felt-tip pen with fine point to trace pattern; cut out pattern. Place pattern on rolled-out dough and use a small, sharp knife to cut out cookies. (*Note:* If dough is sticky, frequently dip knife into flour while cutting out cookies.)

BEATING EGG WHITES

For greatest volume, remove eggs from refrigerator 30 minutes before beating. Beat egg whites in a clean, dry glass bowl.

MELTING CHOCOLATE

To melt chocolate, place chopped or shaved chocolate in top of a double boiler over hot, not simmering, water. Using a dry spoon, stir occasionally until chocolate melts. Remove from heat and use as desired. If chocolate begins to harden, return to heat.

USING CANDY COATING

To melt candy coating, place in top of a double boiler over hot, not simmering, water or in a heavy saucepan over low heat. Using a dry spoon, stir occasionally until coating melts. Remove from heat and use for dipping as desired. If coating begins to harden, return to heat. To flavor candy coating, add a small amount of flavored oil. To thin candy coating, add a small amount of vegetable oil, but no water. To tint candy coating, use an oil-based food coloring.

GENERAL INSTRUCTIONS

ABOUT THE PAPER WE USED

For many of the projects in this book, we used white and colored paper. There are a variety of papers for these projects available at copy centers or craft stores. When selecting paper, choose one that is suitable in weight for the project. We used copier paper, card and cover stock, construction paper, poster board, Bristol board, and handmade paper.

ABOUT ADHESIVES

Refer to the following list when selecting adhesives. Carefully follow the manufacturer's instructions when applying adhesives.

CRAFT GLUE: Recommended for paper, fabric, wood, and floral items. Dry flat or secure with clothespins or straight pins until glue is dry.

FABRIC GLUE: Recommended for fabric or paper items. Dry flat or secure with clothespins or straight pins until glue is dry.

HOT/LOW-TEMPERATURE GLUE GUN AND GLUE STICKS: Recommended for paper, fabric, and floral items; hold in place until set. Dries quickly. Low-temperature glue does not hold as well as hot glue, but offers a safer gluing option.

CRAFT GLUE STICK: Recommended for small, lightweight items. Dry flat.

SPRAY ADHESIVE: Recommended for adhering paper or fabric items. Dry flat.

RUBBER CEMENT: Recommended for adhering paper to paper; dries quickly.

DECOUPAGE GLUE: Recommended for decoupaging fabric or paper pieces to smooth surfaces.

HOUSEHOLD CEMENT: Used for ceramic and metal items; secure until set.

TRACING PATTERNS

Place tracing paper over pattern and trace pattern; cut out. For a more durable pattern, use a permanent pen to trace pattern onto stencil plastic; cut out.

MAKING A TAG

For a quick and easy tag, photocopy desired tag design and color with colored pencils or markers. Use straight-edge or decorative-edge craft scissors to cut out tag; glue to colored paper. Leaving a color border around tag, cut tag from colored paper. Use pen or marker to write message on tag.

For a fabric-backed tag, photocopy desired tag design and color with colored pencils or markers. Use straight-edge or decorative-edge craft scissors to cut out tag. Use pen or marker to write message on tag. Fuse a piece of paper-backed fusible web to wrong side of fabric. Fuse fabric to poster board. Glue tag to fabric-covered poster board. Leaving a fabric border around tag, cut out tag.

JAR LID FINISHING

1. For jar lid insert, use flat part of a jar lid (same size as jar lid used in storing food) as a pattern and cut one circle each from cardboard, batting, and fabric. Use craft glue to glue batting circle to cardboard circle. Center fabric circle right side up on batting; glue edges of fabric circle to batting.
2. (*Caution:* If jar has been sealed in canning, be careful not to break seal of lid while following Step 2. If seal is broken, jar must be refrigerated.) Just before presenting gift, remove band from filled jar; place jar lid insert in band and replace band over lid.

MAKING A MULTI-LOOP BOW

1. For first streamer, measure desired length of streamer from one end of ribbon; twist ribbon between fingers (Fig. 1).

Fig. 1

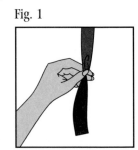

2. Keeping right side of ribbon facing out, fold ribbon to front to form desired-size loop; gather ribbon between fingers (Fig. 2). Fold ribbon to back to form another loop; gather ribbon between fingers (Fig. 3).

Fig. 2   Fig. 3

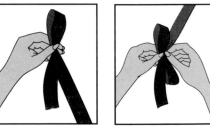

3. (*Note:* If a center loop is desired, form half the desired number of loops, then loosely wrap ribbon around thumb and gather ribbon between fingers as shown in Fig. 4; form remaining loops.) Continue to form loops, varying size of loops as desired, until bow is desired size.

Fig. 4

4. For remaining streamer, trim ribbon to desired length.

5. To secure bow, hold gathered loops tightly. Fold a length of floral wire around gathers of loops. Hold wire ends behind bow, gathering all loops forward; twist bow to tighten wire. Arrange loops and trim ribbon ends as desired.

PAINTING TECHNIQUES

TRANSFERRING PATTERN
Trace pattern onto tracing paper. Using removable tape, tape pattern to project. Place transfer paper coated side down between project and tracing paper. Use a stylus or an old ball point pen that does not write to transfer outlines of basecoat areas of design to project (press lightly to avoid smudges and heavy lines that are difficult to cover). If necessary, use a soft eraser to remove any smudges.

PAINTING BASECOATS
A disposable plate makes a good palette. Use a medium round brush for large areas and a small round brush for small areas. Do not overload brush. Allowing to dry between coats, apply several thin coats of paint to project.

TRANSFERRING DETAILS
To transfer detail lines to design, replace pattern and transfer paper over painted basecoats and use stylus to lightly transfer detail lines onto project.

ADDING DETAILS
Use a permanent pen to draw over detail lines.

SPONGE PAINTING
Use an assembly-line when making several sponge-painted projects. Place project on a covered work surface. Practice sponge-painting technique on scrap paper until desired look is achieved. Paint projects with first color and allow to dry before moving to next color. Use a clean sponge for each additional color.

For allover designs, dip a dampened sponge piece into paint; remove excess paint on a paper towel. Use a light stamping motion to paint item.

For painting with sponge shapes, dip a dampened sponge shape into paint; remove excess paint on a paper towel. Lightly press sponge shape onto project. Carefully lift sponge. For a reverse design, turn sponge shape over.

STENCILING
These instructions are written for multicolor stencils. For single-color stencils, make one stencil for entire design.

1. For first stencil, cut a piece of stencil plastic 1" larger than entire pattern. Center stencil plastic over pattern and use pen to trace outlines of all areas of first color in stencil cutting key. For placement guidelines, outline remaining colored areas with dashed lines. Using a new piece of stencil plastic for each additional color in stencil cutting key, repeat for remaining stencils.

2. Use a craft knife and cutting mat to cut out stencil along solid lines, making sure edges are smooth.

3. Hold or tape stencil in place. Using a clean, dry stencil brush or sponge piece, dip brush or sponge in paint; remove excess paint on a paper towel. Brush or sponge should be almost dry to produce good results. Beginning at edge of cutout area, apply paint in a stamping motion over stencil. If desired, highlight or shade design by stamping a lighter or darker shade of paint in cutout area. Repeat until all areas of first stencil have been painted. Carefully remove stencil and allow paint to dry.

4. Using stencils in order indicated in color key and matching guidelines on stencils to previously stenciled areas, repeat Step 3 for remaining stencils.

5. To stencil a design in reverse, clean stencil, turn stencil over, and repeat Steps 3 and 4.

MAKING APPLIQUÉS

Follow all steps for each appliqué. When tracing patterns for more than one appliqué, leave at least 1" between shapes on web.

To make a reverse appliqué, trace pattern onto tracing paper, turn traced pattern over, and follow all steps using traced pattern.

1. Trace appliqué pattern onto paper side of web. Cutting about 1/2" outside drawn lines, cut out web shape.

2. Follow manufacturer's instructions to fuse web shape to wrong side of fabric. Cut out shape along drawn lines.

MAKING A SEWN FABRIC BAG

1. To determine width of fabric needed, add 1/2" to desired finished width of bag. To determine length of fabric needed, double desired finished height of bag and add 1 1/2". Cut a piece of fabric the determined measurements.

2. With right sides together and matching short edges, fold fabric in half; finger press folded edge (bottom of bag). Using a 1/4" seam allowance, sew sides of bag together.

Continued on page 124

GENERAL INSTRUCTIONS (continued)

3. For bag with flat bottom, match each side seam to fold line at bottom of bag; sew across each corner 1" from point (Fig. 1).

Fig. 1

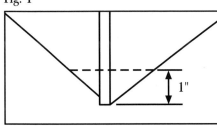

4. Press top edge of bag ¹⁄₄" to wrong side; press ¹⁄₂" to wrong side again and stitch in place.

5. Turn bag right side out.

MAKING A BASKET LINER

For liner with an unfinished edge, cut or tear a fabric piece ¹⁄₄" larger on all sides than desired finished size of liner. Fringe edges of fabric piece ¹⁄₄" or use pinking shears to trim edges.

For liner with a finished edge, cut a fabric piece ¹⁄₂" larger on all sides than desired finished size of liner. Press edges of fabric piece ¹⁄₄" to wrong side; press ¹⁄₄" to wrong side again and stitch in place.

COVERING A BOX

Use this technique to cover cardboard boxes that are unassembled or are easily unfolded, such as pie boxes.

1. Unfold box to be covered. Cut a piece of wrapping paper 1" larger on all sides than unfolded box. Place wrapping paper right side down on a flat surface.

2. *For a small box,* apply spray adhesive to outside of entire box. Center unfolded box adhesive side down on paper; press firmly to secure. *For a large box,* apply spray adhesive to bottom of box. Center unfolded box adhesive side down on paper; press firmly to secure. Applying spray adhesive to one section at a time, repeat to secure remaining sections of box to paper.

3. Use a craft knife to cut paper even with edges of box. If box has slits, use craft knife to cut through slits from inside of box.

4. Reassemble box.

CROSS STITCH

COUNTED CROSS STITCH(X)

Work one Cross Stitch to correspond to each colored square in chart. For horizontal rows, work stitches in two journeys (Fig. 1). For vertical rows, complete each stitch as shown in Fig. 2.

Fig. 1

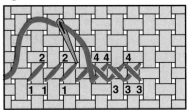

Fig. 2

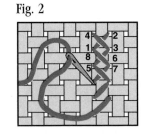

BACKSTITCH(B'ST)

For outline detail, Backstitch (shown in chart and color key by black or colored straight lines) should be worked after design has been completed (Fig. 3).

Fig. 3

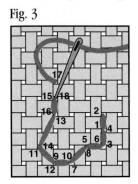

EMBROIDERY

FRENCH KNOT

Bring needle up at 1 (Fig. 1); wrap floss once around needle and insert needle at 2, holding end of floss with non-stitching fingers. Tighten knot, then pull needle through fabric, holding floss until it must be released. For a larger knot, use more strands; wrap only once.

Fig. 1

RUNNING STITCH

Make a series of straight stitches with stitch length equal to the space between stitches (Fig. 2).

Fig. 2

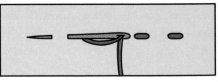

RECIPE INDEX

A

Almond-Amaretto Turtles, 55
APPETIZERS AND SNACKS:
Autumn Popcorn Mix, 95
Birthday Party Treats, 20
Crunchy Granola Snack Mix, 23
Crunchy Popcorn Mix, 82
Do-Daddy Snack Mix, 57
Earth Day Snack Mix, 36
Easter Bunny Treats, 38
Halloween Snack Mix, 89
Honey-Mustard Cheese Spread, 12
Meat Jerky, 77
Orange Popcorn Balls, 88
Radish Dip with Rye Chips, 72
Rosewater Spread, 46
Spicy Popcorn Seasoning, 35
Tangy Peach Salsa, 65
Tasty Catfish Spread, 66
Toffee-Sprinkled Pretzels, 107
Veggie Dip, 74
Apricot Cider, 98
Apricot-Walnut Rugelach, 101
April Fools' Candy, 34
Artists' Cookie Crayons, 24
Autumn Popcorn Mix, 95

B

BEVERAGES:
Apricot Cider, 98
Fiesta Punch Mix, 44
Fresh Mint Lemonade, 62
Herb Tea Blend, 9
Lemon-Raspberry Sleepy Tea Mix, 48
Raspberry Champagne Cocktails, 8
Spicy Cocoa Mix, 13
Strawberry-Vanilla Drink Mix, 100
Birdhouse Cookies, 22
Birthday Party Treats, 20
Black Walnut Brittle, 106
Bologna and Cheese Sandwich Spread, 74

BREADS AND MUFFINS:
Casserole Herb Bread, 45
Irish Soda Bread Mix, 92
Red-White-and-Blue Muffins, 64
Vegetable Roll-Up Bread
with Pesto Spread, 53

C

CAKES AND CUPCAKES:
Fudgy Chocolate Chip Cupcakes, 97
Mini Chocolate-Mint Cheesecakes, 47
Orange Slice Cakes, 103
Springtime Cake, 43
Strawberry Sweetheart Cakes, 19
CANDIES:
Almond-Amaretto Turtles, 55
April Fools' Candy, 34
Black Walnut Brittle, 106
Chocolate Cherry-Almond Creams, 16
Chocolate-Peanut Butter Candies, 90
Cookies and Cream Candies, 85
Herb Candies, 70
Minty Chocolate Creams, 26
Orange-Mocha Coffee Beans, 39
Casserole Herb Bread, 45
Cheese Blend, 15
Cheesy Potato-Sausage Soup, 6
Cherry Honey, 81
Chilled Garden Soup, 63
Chocolate Cherry-Almond Creams, 16
Chocolate Fudge Pie, 71
Chocolate-Peanut Butter Candies, 90
Chocolate Slice and Bake Cookies, 74
Coconut Bird Nests, 28
CONDIMENTS:
Cheese Blend, 15
Cherry Honey, 81
Creamy Fresh Salsa, 15
Easy Hot Dog Relish, 58
Green Tomato Relish, 76
Herbed Butters, 50
Mustard Relish, 15
Onion Relish, 15

Pear Honey, 102
Snappy Strawberry-Jalapeño Sauce, 37
Spicy Carrot-Orange Conserve, 78
Tangy Peach Salsa, 65
Cookies and Cream Candies, 85
COOKIES, BARS, AND BROWNIES:
Apricot-Walnut Rugelach, 101
Artists' Cookie Crayons, 24
Birdhouse Cookies, 22
Chocolate Slice and Bake Cookies, 74
Coconut Bird Nests, 28
Golf Ball Cookies, 29
Jumbo Walnut-Chocolate Chunk
Cookies, 87
Pot of Gold Cookies, 27
Pumpkin Cookies, 93
Spicy Christmas Tree Cookies, 105
Straw Hat Cookies, 30
Strawberry Cheesecake Bars, 84
Creamy Fresh Salsa, 15
Creamy Peanut Butter Pie, 21
Crunchy Granola Snack Mix, 23
Crunchy Popcorn Mix, 82

D

DESSERTS (See also Cakes and Cupcakes; Candies; Cookies, Bars, and Brownies; Fudge; Pies):
Grand Marnier Baklava, 31
Tropical Fruit Sherbet, 61
Do-Daddy Snack Mix, 57
DRY MIXES AND SEASONINGS:
Herb Tea Blend, 9
Irish Soda Bread Mix, 92
Italian Cracked Pepper Seasoning, 49
Lemon-Raspberry Sleepy Tea Mix, 48
Spicy Cocoa Mix, 13
Spicy Popcorn Seasoning, 35
Strawberry-Vanilla Drink Mix, 100

Continued on page 126

RECIPE INDEX (continued)

CREDITS

To Magna IV Color Imaging of Little Rock, Arkansas, we say *thank you* for the superb color reproduction and excellent pre-press preparation.

We want to especially thank photographers Larry Pennington, Mark Mathews, and Ken West of Peerless Photography, Little Rock, Arkansas, for their time, patience, and excellent work.

Special thanks go to Duncan and Nancy Porter, who allowed us to photograph some of our foods and projects in their home.

To the talented people who helped in the creation of the following recipe and projects in this book, we extend a special word of thanks:

- *Green Tomato Relish*, page 76: MaryAnn Rohm
- *Cross-Stitch Jar Lid*, page 76: MaryAnn Rohm
- *Christmas Tote*, page 107: Terrie Lee Steinmeyer

We extend a sincere *thank you* to Elaine Garrett and Diana L. Hoke, who assisted in making and testing some of the projects in this book.